BENCH-PRESSED

BENCH-PRESSED

A Judge Recounts the Many Blessings and Heavy Lessons
of Hearing Immigration Asylum Cases

SUSAN L. YARBROUGH

iUniverse, Inc.
Bloomington

Bench-Pressed
A Judge Recounts the Many Blessings and Heavy Lessons of Hearing Immigration Asylum Cases

iUniverse books may be ordered through booksellers or by contacting:

iUniverse
1663 Liberty Drive
Bloomington, IN 47403
www.iuniverse.com
1-800-Authors (1-800-288-4677)

ISBN: 978-1-4759-7542-0 (sc)
ISBN: 978-1-4759-7543-7 (hc)
ISBN: 978-1-4759-7544-4 (e)

Library of Congress Control Number: 2013902420

Printed in the United States of America

iUniverse rev. date: 03/15/2013

For Pam Kaye,

who led me out of Egypt's memories
and gave me asylum.

May your compassion be felt by all.
May your light fill the darkness.
May you be forever blessed.

Contents

Preface

From November 1987 to July 2005, I worked as a United States Immigration Judge primarily in Houston and two other Texas cities but also for short periods in the Washington, DC, area as well as in Florida, Tennessee, Louisiana, and California. Prior to going on the bench, I was an attorney with the New York Legal Aid Society, the New York Attorney General's office, and the United States Attorney's Office for the Southern District of Texas. I also taught Legal Studies and Women's Studies at the University of Massachusetts–Amherst for several years. And in 1993, as part of contemplating a radical career change from law into something kinder and gentler, I went back to school and became a licensed massage therapist.

It was my work as a judge that changed the course of my emotional and spiritual life and prompted me to write this book. At no time during law school, judges' training courses, or thirty years in the legal profession did anyone ever say to me, "Listen with your heart as well as with your ears and your mind," or, "Give careful thought to what is just; then try with all your strength to do it."

But the job of being a judge required me to hear many asylum cases brought by applicants from all over the world, and I knew, even as I was hearing the first case to come before me after I was sworn in, that I would never be the same again. That first case and all the ones that came after it were not cases at all but were living people with their faces pressed up against the glass of the United States, and it was in hearing them tell me what had happened to them in their countries, how they had gotten to my country, and how much they wanted to stay here that gratitude, humility, and the ability to really listen finally took root in me.

During almost eighteen years of judging, I often joked about writing a book entitled *Bench-Pressed* to describe the effect that many asylum narratives had on me. I have trained with weights three times a week since 1970 and have consistently enjoyed both the exertion and the strength benefits, but bench presses have always been the most mentally challenging for me. There is something about lying in a vulnerable supine position on a narrow piece of vinyl-covered board and pushing a heavy metal bar straight toward the ceiling that seems dangerously gravity-defying, and if the bar is not carefully controlled, it can come down rapidly and crush the lifter's chest or throat.

Many of the asylum cases that I heard felt like lifting heavy issues vertically from flat on my back, holding their weight aloft for hours, lowering their grief and sadness slowly, peeling myself off the bench at the end of the day, and needing time to recover from the soreness of soul that ensued. At some point after I retired, I remembered the Yiddish word *bentch*, which is loosely translated as "blessing," and I was startled to realize that all the people into whose faces I had looked as they sat on the witness stand near me had indeed blessed me in some way or another. And so a more heartfelt title of this book could easily have been *Bentch-Pressed*.

Because the words *blessing* and *spiritual* seem to be so frequently and carelessly bandied about without much definition, I considered them carefully before using either of them in the title or in the text. Both words have personal historical and emotional meaning for me, but I thought it important to formulate some accessible working definitions to hold in mind while writing.

Blessing seems to be a multipurpose word we use to connote something beneficial that is given or received, or approval of some sort (as in "you have my blessing"). We also use it in ways that sound remedial or medicinal, as in blessing someone who has just sneezed, or as we do in the South, saying "bless your heart" when we find out that someone has experienced some difficulty or loss. I usually think of a blessing in the first sense—as some intangible positive that one soul gives to another.

American writer and lecturer David Spangler, who at one time codirected the spiritual community of Findhorn in northern Scotland, has observed that blessings "need not be actions or events at all. They can be subtle influences that embrace us, moving invisibly in our lives to empower, support, and nourish us." Moreover, blessings can force us to change, to look at our lives in new ways, and to discover possibilities we wouldn't have noticed before; and their primary effect is to liberate us by giving us "something—support, vitality, insight, opportunity—to enhance and expand our lives." Most importantly, receiving a blessing awakens the giver in us and lifts us "in gratitude and delight" to an awareness that we are connected to each other and are "part of a larger whole."[1] I understand these words, for I know that what I received from those who asked me for asylum has changed me, freed me, and connected me to others in ways I never even imagined were possible.

The word *spiritual* presents even more definitional challenges, and I was recently amused to hear a clergy friend report the results of a survey showing that the fastest growing denomination in America is SBNR, i.e., Spiritual But Not Religious. Jungian psychoanalyst Lionel Corbett notes that our spirituality is "our way of understanding the nature of things ... [and] is reflected in our values, in the way we pursue significance, and sometimes in a sense that there is an unseen, subtle realm of existence that orders our lives." Thus, "We use the term *spirituality* to mean an individual or private sense of the sacred, rather than an institutional approach that adheres to particular doctrine and dogma, a defined system of theology, [or] prescribed rituals."[2]

I like the observation of author and journalist Dan Wakefield that spirituality expresses itself "in care for family, friends and fellow human beings, in the passion for learning and perfecting one's craft, for enjoying and appreciating the commonplace gifts of everyday experience and finding in them the inspiration for living more fully."[3] And I have also seen spirituality express itself in social activism.

For purposes of what I have written in the pages that follow, my inner emphasis has been on spirituality as a pursuit of significance, as a relationship to the unseen, and as a private sense of the sacred— in other words, my subjective knowledge and feelings about the connection between the self and the transcendent, especially as they increasingly evidenced themselves in my approach to my work as a judge.

In 1978, I was a student in a challenging adult education course at a synagogue on Manhattan's Upper West Side. Many people in the class were attorneys, and discussions were often about the dynamic tension between *din* and *rachamim*—justice and mercy. To the extent that there was any consensus of ideas, most participants seemed to agree that a legal system based solely on justice is perforce a harsh and unforgiving one, while a system based solely on mercy would be sorely lacking in order, predictability, and accountability. These energetic discussions and provocative ideas have continued to affect me over the years. I thought of them every day I was on the bench, and as I tried to yoke them to the concept of walking with humility before God and my fellow human beings, I began to see and feel many parts of my work as an expression of my own spirituality.

The third term that warrants some definition is *soul*. Greek-born philosopher and psychologist Evangelos Christou wrote a monumental work about the soul,[4] but I found it impenetrable when I read it many years ago. Recently, however, I saw an especially helpful theoretical summary of Christou's work. According to the commentator, Christou views the realm of soul as "the realm of meaning that is discovered when we look into ourselves, when we are inspired or deeply affected by music, art, ritual, a person, the natural world, by love or beauty ... The soul is about what matters to us."[5]

I use the term *soul* very infrequently in this book, but when I do, it refers to how I was affected by those who testified before me and how they mattered to and inspired me then and now. They often spoke to me in what sounded like poetry, and the poignancy of it still shakes my soul very hard.

Several of the principles of my own Jewish faith were always in my consciousness when I worked as a judge: the *mitzvah* (commandment) to welcome the stranger, as well as the admonition to do justly, love mercy, and walk humbly with God. In constructing this book, I have also been mindful of two important verbs within my faith: *remember* and *tell*, which are often used in the context of the Exodus and the Holocaust.

The stories here are all true, although I have changed the names of the tellers and a number of other identifying details (including the cities in which I heard them) in order to protect them and their privacy as they make new lives in this regrettably tell-all American society. Each of them endured torture and persecution of many kinds, all of it horrific, and they deserve to have their lives remembered and told if for no other reason than the hope that war, atrocities, and the intolerance born of fear-based hatred for "the other" will someday end.

On several occasions I have heard established authors say that every story is in fact two stories—that of the author as well as that of the subject—and that we write to make order out of chaos. It would be disingenuous for me not to admit that I have written this book in part to tell my own story and thereby foster my own catharsis and healing. As nineteenth-century novelist Isak Dinesen was once said to have observed, "All sorrows can be borne if you put them into a story or tell a story about them."[6] And as contemporary writer and conservationist Terry Tempest Williams has more recently noted, "I write to make peace with the things I cannot control ... I write to the questions that shatter my sleep."[7]

When I left my job in the summer of 2005 at the age of fifty-eight pursuant to an early-retirement package offered to all those who met certain requirements of age and years of service, little did I know that I would almost immediately begin spewing nightmares and symptoms of secondary post-traumatic stress disorder like contrails from a jumbo jet. Reading, rest, meditation, prayer, writing, and the blessing of a gifted therapist have settled me enormously, and I have needed to write this book in order to move on with my life.

I was both strengthened and softened by my job. Because of my experiences in it, I feel at home in the world, and I look for opportunities to help strangers feel welcome. I am a changed and better person for having done this work for over half of my thirty years in the legal profession, and I am profoundly grateful for having been allowed to see and hear and feel all I did while I was listening to other people tell me about their lives and their hopes.

For those who spoke their truth and gave me the lasting blessing of connectedness, thanks always, and all ways.

Introduction

United States Immigration Court proceedings are quite different from the civil and criminal trials with which the American public is familiar by virtue of direct experience or media exposure. There is no jury, and all cases are decided by the judge alone.

As with any specialized area of law, immigration law and procedure have their own idioms and idiosyncrasies. These I have briefly highlighted in this section in order for the reader to more fully understand the context in which the asylum cases in this book arose. I have also included information about my own methodology in putting the book together and have provided a preview of how each chapter is internally structured.

At the outset, it is very important to note that at the time I heard the cases described in this book, the United States Immigration Courts were *not* part of the former Immigration and Naturalization Service (INS), nor are they now a part of its successor agency, Immigration and Customs Enforcement (ICE).

Terminology

When I first began working as a judge in 1987, a person was brought before the immigration court pursuant to a charging document called an *order to show cause* that listed the various grounds on which the US government was seeking to deport the person, such as his or her having entered the United States illegally or having committed a crime while here. The person before the court was referred to as a *respondent,* because he or she would be required to respond to the charges of deportability and to show cause why he or she should not be deported.

After significant changes in the law in 1996, the terms *deportation* and *deportation proceedings* were replaced with *removal* and *removal proceedings.* The government was represented by what was then called the Immigration and Naturalization Service (INS). After a massive reorganization of that agency in early 2002, the INS became Immigration and Customs Enforcement (ICE), one of the major components of the Department of Homeland Security.

Because all the cases I describe in this book were heard prior to 1996, I will use the older and more familiar terms *INS* to designate the prosecuting authority and its attorney and *deportation* to indicate the nature of the proceedings and the unsuccessful outcome for many respondents.

A respondent's first appearance in immigration court takes place at a *master calendar hearing* that is much like an arraignment docket in criminal court. At the master calendar, the United States immigration judge advises the respondent of his or her rights, and the respondent is entitled to a continuance in order to obtain counsel.

When the respondent returns to court for a second master calendar appearance, he or she is expected to plead to the charges of deportability. If the judge finds that the charges are sustainable and that the respondent is deportable, the respondent must designate a country to which he or she wishes to be deported if deportation becomes necessary. The judge then determines if there is any statutory relief from deportation (such as asylum) that might be available to the respondent. If so, the court sets a date for the application to be filed as well as a date for a hearing on the merits of the application.

Because of the enormous number of cases on the dockets handled by US immigration judges, it is not unusual for a respondent to wait at least a year for a hearing on his or her application for relief from deportation.

Definitions

There have been a number of changes in asylum law since I heard the five cases included in this book, but the basics remain the same.

A person seeking to qualify for asylum must establish that he or she is unable or unwilling to return to his or her country because of past persecution or a well-founded fear (i.e., a reasonable probability) of future persecution. The persecution must be by the government or a group that the government cannot control, and it must be on account of at least one of five statutory grounds: the respondent's race, religion, nationality, membership in a particular social group, or political opinion.

Persecution is not defined in the Immigration and Nationality Act but has been interpreted by the courts to mean harm, threats, or physical abuse of a serious nature and not mere harassment. Because the past persecution or the feared future persecution must be on account of one of the five grounds and must also have been perpetrated by the government or a group that the government cannot control, cases that involve privately motivated street crimes, discrimination, or domestic abuse generally do not fall within the scope of US asylum law.

Once the asylum applicant has established past persecution or a well-founded fear of future persecution based on one of the five grounds, the burden then shifts to the government to prove by a preponderance of the evidence that the person is not eligible for asylum. This is generally done by showing that there have been fundamental changes in the applicant's country of nationality (such as the end of a war) or that the applicant can avoid harm by relocating to another part of his or her country.

Court Procedure

Immigration court proceedings are commonly referred to as being civil proceedings, and although respondents are entitled to many of the rights of criminal defendants (such as cross-examination and confrontation of the witnesses against them), they are not entitled to have an attorney appointed to represent them. Many US immigration judges regard the proceedings as more quasicriminal than civil in nature.

Unfortunately, many attorneys who specialize in other areas of the law (such as criminal defense) believe that they can easily segue into immigration court and adequately represent respondents facing deportation proceedings. Immigration law, however, is as complicated as the Internal Revenue Code, and I would frequently have to admonish would-be crossover attorneys (including one who candidly admitted that this was his "first rodeo in immigration court after doin' only DWI cases for the past thirty years") that their civil clients would pay fines, their criminal clients would go to jail, but their immigration clients would suffer worst of all because *they* would be deported. Moreover, notwithstanding the softer terminology of *respondents* and *civil proceedings*, immigration court proceedings are highly adversarial and, especially in the case of a respondent who is represented by an attorney, often replete with lengthy documents and exhibits and a substantial witness list.

The majority of respondents I saw in court could not afford to hire an attorney, so they proceeded pro se, representing themselves as best they could. Typically, their asylum applications were incomplete and sketchy and had usually been prepared by someone else with minimal skills in the English language.

In court, respondents were provided with interpreters in their own languages. Interpreters were either permanent employees of the court or were contracted for by the court through a commercial interpretation service, such as Berlitz. In cases where a respondent's language was not widely spoken (such as Miskito, which is spoken by some indigenous people on the northeastern coast of Nicaragua, or Quiché, which is spoken by Mayan descendants in the central highlands of Guatemala), competent interpreters were scarce and often had to be flown in from other parts of the United States, resulting in lengthy delays before proceedings could be firmly scheduled.

The pro se cases were by far the most difficult of all for me to handle. Because it was my responsibility to be impartial, I obviously could not represent the respondents as an advocate, but neither could I in good conscience let them sit mute and mystified while the government's attorney rolled over them like a juggernaut. So, like many other immigration judges, I developed simplistic ways of cuing respondents about what to do, saying things like, "This is the time in court when you can tell me what happened to your family when the soldiers came through your village," or, "You now have the right to ask the INS officer questions to be sure that he is telling the truth"—verbal tracer bullets fired in the hope that they would shed some light that could be followed to a testimonial target.

Most respondents, whether represented by counsel or not, were clearly frightened of court proceedings, and I would frequently hear statements like, "The tribunal in my country was held under a tent in the jungle," or, "Trials in my country are by dossier, and I didn't get to say anything before I got sent to prison."

It is strange and bittersweet to work at the center of a system heavily weighted against someone without an attorney or even the statutory right to one but to realize that this system is somehow less oppressive than many.[8]

Methodology and Organization

In my first year as an attorney, an exceptional and experienced colleague told me that 98 percent of the practice of law is routine, and over the next twelve years of my own practice, I found this to be true.

During my almost eighteen years as a judge, many immigration cases sounded much the same, and this was especially so as, one by one, Central American countries not all that far from Houston emptied out due to poverty and civil war. I tried not to treat the thousands of cases on my docket every year as routine, but the applications and pretrial paperwork submitted to me in many of them were frequently so insubstantial that my preparation would consist of perhaps only an hour or so of reading.

In other cases, however, I could tell from the application or supporting documentation that an unusually strong claim was being made, and I spent many hours in preparation for those cases. United States immigration courts have never provided a law clerk for each judge, so I generally prepared my own bench memos, which were organized narrative summaries of what the case was about and what questions and legal issues needed to addressed in the course of the hearing.

During the hearing itself, I took copious notes that I used to formulate either oral decisions rendered from the bench or written decisions composed after a period of deliberation. Unless the losing party took an appeal, I never saw the transcript of a hearing and certainly did not photocopy any I did see. Over the years, I saved the bench memos and hearing notes that I generated before and during the most difficult—and therefore the most instructive—cases I heard. I did not make or keep copies of any asylum applications.

Thus, in constructing this book, I have relied solely on my bench memos and hearing notes as well as my own memory about what was testified to in court. Because I do not have transcripts of the hearings and the sworn testimonies contained in them, my accounts of the five cases that follow might, in some respects, be viewed as what literati are now calling "creative nonfiction," a term I first saw only after I had finished writing the five chapters of this book. The genre has been defined in different ways by various authors, two of whom describe it as "fact-based writing ... that has at heart an interest in enduring human values ..."[9] This was certainly my goal when I began to write, and I hope I have achieved it, even though I think this book is more accurately classified as a memoir based on facts that I have chosen to make essentially unverifiable in order to protect the identities, the privacy, and the safety of those whose stories are at the heart of it. Even as far back as a century and a half ago, Emily Dickinson well understood the subtle power of this kind of storytelling when she advised writers to "Tell all the Truth but tell it slant," for "Truth must dazzle gradually / Or every man be blind."[10]

Each of the five chapters in this book has three sections. The first is a brief background history of the country from which the asylum applicant fled. The second is an account of what happened in court and the testimony that I heard.

When someone is asked to verbally recount a traumatic experience, he or she will often begin to speak of it in fits and starts, backing and filling as different nuances of the experience surface in memory. The testimony of these five respondents came rushing out with an urgency that did not neatly separate itself into paragraphs or an orderly chronology, and it was always a challenge to rearrange their narratives into a coherent account for purposes not only of making a decision on the facts but also of incorporating a summary of their testimony into the oral or written decision I issued in the case.

The third section of each chapter is a personal reflection about the thoughts, memories, and emotions that arose in me in response to the life of the applicant, and about the ongoing lessons and blessings I received and am still receiving because of listening to a person who risked everything in search of freedom and peace and safety.

Four of the asylum applicants in this book came from Spanish-speaking countries, and I have therefore referred to them here—and as I did in court according to the manners and customs of their countries—by their matronymic names (usually the first of their two surnames).

Finally, because I wanted the background section of each case to read easily and the voices and stories of those for whom I am speaking to flow with little interruption, I have avoided the use of legal citations throughout, have used footnotes only sparingly, and have not attempted any thoroughgoing explication of politics or geopolitics. In other words, this is not a scholarly book, but rather it is one for the reader who wants to know more about the lives and faces behind the daily swirl of polarized and emotionally charged debates about immigration in the United States.

The law refers to people who come here illegally as *aliens,* and many US citizens (and even some immigration judges) believe that most of them have come to commit crimes or to take unfair advantage of medical, educational, and social services. This was not my experience at all. To be sure, some people enter the United States surreptitiously for illicit purposes, but the overwhelming majority of those who appeared before me in court came here simply to work and to help their families. And apart from these many economic refugees, there were and are many people who come to this country because they have been greatly harmed in their own countries, and they are the ones about whom I have chosen to write.

To refresh my memory about the countries from which the asylees in this book came, I began with the convenience of online sources, and from there I proceeded to check and recheck facts and information using a variety of other materials, such as hard-copy encyclopedias, articles from reputable newspapers and wire services, the Country Reports issued by the United States Department of State every year about every country in the world, and the yearly reports of Amnesty International and other established and reliable human rights organizations.

It is not my intent to provide any legal authority or advice, and any errors in law, dates, or facts are entirely my own. Where I thought it important or useful to explain something within the asylum applicant's narrative, I have generally done so within brackets, and I have also tried to ensure that the meaning of any non-English word or phrase is made clear in the text immediately following its use.

Although I have often come close in this book to reproducing the actual testimony given in court, I could never begin to reproduce either the anguish that each of the applicants conveyed or the dignity and lack of self-pity with which each one conveyed it. The durability of their souls—and the plainness and simplicity of their speech—never failed to move me, and they continue to do so to this day.

My wish, indeed my continuing passion,
would be not to point the finger in judgment but to part a curtain,
that invisible shadow that falls between people,
the veil of indifference to each other's presence,
each other's wonder,
each other's human plight.

—Eudora Welty

Here *is the time for the sayable:* here *is its homeland.*
Speak and bear witness.

—Rainer Maria Rilke

If they tell you there is wisdom among the nations,
believe them.

—Lamentations Rabbah 2, 9:13

1. Persecution on Account of Race: Esteban Marcial Mosqueda of Cuba

Background

The island now called Cuba was discovered by Christopher Columbus during his voyage to the New World in 1492. By 1514 the Spanish Empire had colonized the island after brutal suppression and massacres of the indigenous people, who were understandably reluctant to work for their new European masters. In the absence of a ready and willing pool of laborers, the Spanish eventually began importing slaves from Africa to work in the burgeoning and profitable tobacco, sugar cane, and coal-mining industries—a practice that continued until slavery was abolished in Cuba in 1886.

Except for a short period in the eighteenth century when it was held by Great Britain, Cuba was ruled by Spanish governors until it gained independence in 1902 following four years of United States occupation at the end of the Spanish-American War in 1898. For the next four decades, Cuba democratically elected a series of presidents, many of whom proved ineffective in dealing with the corruption that arose in response to increased prosperity. After World War II, Cuba enjoyed a boom in its economy, health services, and educational opportunities, but many of these gains were undermined by the government of Fulgencio Batista, who had been elected president in 1953.

1

On January 1, 1959, under pressure from the United States and a growing number of opposition citizen and guerrilla groups within Cuba, Batista fled the country. Backed by his own followers as well as other rebel armies and groups that had been gathering with him in the mountains, Fidel Castro stepped into the void. Six days later, the United States recognized the Castro government and sent a new ambassador to the island.

Within months of seizing power, however, Castro purged all of his political opponents (and even some of his supporters), took over the media and schools, and instituted a one-party Communist system that brooked no opposition or questions. By the summer of 1959, the stunned Eisenhower administration began planning the ouster of Fidel Castro, and relations between the two countries deteriorated rapidly as it became apparent from his public statements that the new dictator wanted nothing to do with the United States.

Soon after his inauguration in January 1961, President John F. Kennedy authorized the notorious Bay of Pigs invasion in which a US-trained force of approximately 1,300 Cuban exiles invaded the southern coast of Cuba with the intention of overthrowing the Castro government. Castro's armed forces defeated the invaders within three days.

In October 1962, in what became known as the Cuban Missile Crisis, the United States successfully cordoned off international waters in order to prevent the Soviet Union from sending into Cuba more missiles than those previously discovered in U-2 reconnaissance photos. Soviet economic aid, however, continued to pour into Cuba until the final collapse of the Soviet Union in 1991.

Left largely unchecked either by any internal voice of reason or by the Soviet Union, the Communist Party of Fidel Castro began imprisoning moderates and members of the middle class in forced labor camps soon after it came to power. Many Cubans of European descent who could afford to leave the island did so, and as the economy declined, unemployment soared.

In 1972, the Castro government instituted an anti-loafing law that made it a crime to be a working-age male without a job. Those caught not working could either go to jail or go fight in Soviet-backed wars on the African continent in Angola, Algeria, Congo, and Ethiopia.

While slavery had been abolished in Cuba in 1886, prejudice had not, and although the black population of Cuba increased enormously over the next seventy-five years, it remained at the bottom of the social and job structure and was viewed as inferior by those of European descent who controlled the government and the economy. Additionally, as the United States became more invested in Cuba politically and economically, it tacitly endorsed the ideological and attitudinal apartheid on the island and did as little to promote racial equality there as it did within its own borders.

By the time of the Castro revolution in 1959, an estimated 60 to 70 percent of the Cuban population was of African or mixed African heritage and thus obviously outnumbered those who were of strictly Spanish or European descent. Initially, many Afro-Cubans supported the revolution, believing its egalitarian promises of land reform, better education, and adequate health care and social services. And even though matters did seem to improve superficially in the early years of the regime, Castro made it very clear that the primary goal of his revolution was to eliminate distinctions in class rather than in race.

As Euro-Cubans and their money fled postrevolutionary Cuba, they left behind a crumbling economy, an iron-fisted dictator, and a majority Afro-Cuban underclass that had little money, few resources, no power, and absolutely no avenue for the redress of their grievances. One of the repressive tools of the Castro government was the formation of Committees for the Defense of the Revolution

(CDRs) that were (and still are) block-watch groups charged with reporting any allegedly counterrevolutionary speech or activity to the government.

In order to survive, many Afro-Cubans resorted to buying and selling goods on the black market, and some would occasionally question obvious racial disparities in housing or employment. Both of these activities, along with penalties for violating the anti-loafing law, caused the imprisonment of Afro-Cubans in numbers far disproportionate to even their majority status.

In early April 1980, starting with a small group and eventually swelling to 10,000 citizens, Cubans seeking asylum from their own government stormed the Peruvian embassy in Havana. In response, Fidel Castro announced that any Cuban who wished to leave the country could do so through the port of Mariel. From April 15 to the end of October, there was a mass exodus of approximately 125,000 Cubans, most of whom traveled by boats and rafts to the United States. The Cuban government also saw fit to release many Cubans who were in prisons and mental hospitals and to direct or transport them to the port. A large percentage of those released from institutions were Afro-Cubans. Castro labeled all who departed Cuba "undesirables" and "scum."

As a matter of general policy, the United States government did not seek to deport or repatriate anyone who had fled postrevolutionary Cuba unless he or she had been convicted of a crime in that country.

In Court

Esteban Marcial Mosqueda entered the courtroom for his asylum hearing in July 1991 with an able attorney. He had not had one when he first appeared before me a year earlier at a master calendar, and when I picked up his file to start preparations a few days before the hearing, I was pleased to see that an experienced lawyer had taken his case pro bono.

Attorneys who specialize in immigration law seldom enter that area of practice to grow wealthy or famous, and many of them are good-hearted but overworked individuals who grew up in immigrant families and want to honor that part of their heritage. When I first started working as a judge, I would sometimes try to cajole a solo practitioner into taking a meritorious case for free, appealing to his or her moral (if not legal) obligation under the code of ethics to do some pro bono work. But I soon stopped doing that, because I had doubts about whether judicial ethics permitted my predetermining which cases could be developed into winners with the assistance of counsel and which did not warrant an attorney's efforts.

Mr. Marcial was in deportation proceedings because he had been convicted in his country of the crime of loafing. Thus, unlike noncriminal Cubans, he was ineligible to pursue US residency a year after his arrival in the United States and was therefore required to seek asylum if he wished to remain here. His asylum application was clear and coherent, and it stated that the basis of his claim was persecution based on race.

In my almost four years on the bench, I had not heard a race-based asylum case, nor did I know much about Cuba other than what mainstream American media had reported since Castro came to power in 1959. During a brief period in the late 1970s when Cuba was temporarily open to American visitors, a few of my students at the University of Massachusetts had traveled there with a professor in the Afro-American Studies program, and I had heard from them only glowing reports about how the revolution had transformed all aspects of that country. So at a minimum, I looked forward to hearing Mr. Marcial's case not only because he had a skilled attorney but also because it would be another learning experience for me.

I remembered Mr. Marcial from his first court appearance a year earlier because he was so black. When I had worked for the New York Legal Aid Society, several of my clients had been black Puerto Ricans, so the concept of black Latinos was not new to me. Mr. Marcial, however, was the darkest Latino I had ever seen, and if I had not known he was Cuban, I would have thought that he was from Africa.

Unlike many asylum applicants from Central America, he was not deferential, although he was polite. I was aware that many Cubans have at least high school educations and are proud of their command of the Spanish language, and I had noticed that the original handwritten affidavit accompanying Mr. Marcial's asylum application—even though it had later been translated and word-processed by his attorney—was literate in its own right.

There were several pieces of supporting documentation, each of which pointed to ongoing racism and racial discrimination in postrevolutionary Cuba. Under United States asylum law, however, not every instance of discrimination or unfair treatment is viewed as persecution, and I was therefore especially interested in how this case might unfold. It began in this matter-of-fact way:

> I am Esteban Marcial Mosqueda, the only son of Ana Gutierrez Marcial and Félix Sotolongo Mosqueda. I was born in Havana, country of Cuba, on June 4, 1960, and I completed high school in 1978. My father died that summer. He was a porter. My mother was a maid. She died last year, and I was not there to bury her. I was still an infant when the revolution came, so I do not remember it. But my mother and my father talked about it often and told me there was dancing in the streets. *Todos los negros* [all the black people] thought their lives would change.
>
> In school I learned about Fidel and what he did for us, and even though my grades were good, my classmates

laughed at me because I am so dark. One of them called me a *mambí* [a somewhat derogatory reference to black guerrilla fighters who rebelled against the Spanish Empire in the nineteenth century], and when I told this to my father, he swore and told me to be strong. I had hoped to go to university, but when he died, I knew I had to work.

I took the paper with my grades and started asking everywhere for jobs. My mother was still working, but she had problems with her heart. I lived with her in an apartment smaller than this courtroom. Many things were wrong with it. I wanted to make money to fix it up and let her quit her job. I walked around the city every day and went in bakeries and butcher shops asking for work. One of the owners said he would never let someone as black as me work for him. Then I tried a few small stores that sell used clothing, but no one had a job for me.

By October, I was desperate. I saw my mother was not well, and I made an appointment for her at the clinic. They told her to come back in six months. I begged for them to see her sooner, but they reported me to the CDR in my neighborhood for making elitist demands. A few days later I asked for a job cutting sugar cane in the fields, but the boss said he had heard I was a troublemaker, so I gave up hope.

I knew someone who did illegal things. He would go into the countryside and buy eggs from a peasant for a very low price and then sell them on the black market for a profit. The thought of doing things like this scared me, but it was all I had. So I worked for him and made a few pesos to help my mother.

In May of the next year [1979], I was walking home along a busy street, and the police jumped out at me. They demanded my identity card, and I showed it to them. They asked me where I worked, but I did not want to get my friend in trouble, so I told them I was looking for a job. They told me I was a criminal because I did not have a job, and they took me to the police station and held me for six hours and called me *mancha el negro* [stained black man]. These were Fidel's police!

I begged them to let me go home to my mother, and they finally pushed me out the door. After this, I was too scared to go back to work with my friend, so I stayed at home during the day and went out at night looking for food. I thought if I could find some, my mother would not have to buy it for us. I looked in garbage cans for many months and sometimes found part of a banana or some chicken pieces but never very much. *Así es.* That's the way it is.

Everywhere you go in Cuba there are signs that say *No hay racismo aquí* [There is no racism here] and *Somos uno* [We are one]. These are lies. I kept looking for food at night, and in January [now 1980] I fell asleep in a doorway just before dawn. I woke up when the police kicked me, and once again they took me to jail. They called me a *vagabundo* [bum] and looked up my file. This was the second time, and they knew it. I was shaking.

They told me I could join the army and go to Angola to fight with other *negros*, or I could go to prison. This was not a hard choice for me. Go somewhere and die, or stay here and hope to see my mother again? I chose prison, and they laughed and said I would be sorry. They put me in jail and gave me a trial. I was convicted of violating the law against being unemployed, and my sentence was five years in prison.

A few weeks later, they took me from the jail in Havana to Melena II [a prison in Havana province]. Nobody here believes me, but there are almost a thousand prisons in my country. [Many observers of Cuba have described the prison system of that small island as a gulag consisting of hundreds of prisons.] I was thrown into a cell with other *negros*, and the sergeant could not stop staring at me. He frightened me with his looks.

There were no beds and no sheets, so I slept on the floor with the other men. The toilet was a hole in the floor, and it overflowed every day. At night the rats and roaches came through it, and sometimes a snake. Our food was beans once a day, and it was always filled with insects and worms. We got a pail of water every other day; it was for drinking, but it was so dirty it made us sick.

After I had been there for a week, the sergeant called for me one night. I wondered if I was being released to go to my mother, but that was not it. In his private office, the sergeant told me he had never seen a Cuban so black, and he wanted to know if my penis was as black as my face. While he pointed his gun at me, I let my pants fall. He picked up my private parts and held them in his hands and said, *Hola pendejo negro, cómo está?* Hello, black dumbass. How are you? After that he squeezed my testicles, tied me to a chair, and said he had some surgery to perform.

For several hours after that, he pulled out all my pubic hairs with tweezers, laughing and saying he was soon to be transferred to another prison and he wanted a souvenir of the blackest Cuban he had ever seen. When it was over, he poured liquor on my crotch, told me to get my clothes, and shoved me all the way back to my cell. I tried to tell the other men what had happened, but I could not speak.

I don't remember the next days and weeks, but I must have stayed in the cell. After I was myself again, I thought of

9

my mother all the time and wondered if I could escape. The others told me I would be killed if I tried. My father came to me in dreams at night and told me to be strong.

Many months and many guards went by. All of them would stare at me, and most of them would call me *negro azul* [bluish-black negro, referring to the deep hue of his skin] and have a look at my penis. I was very thin by then, and it was easy for them to pull down my pants.

On my twentieth birthday, I did not want to live anymore, and I decided to go on a hunger strike. My companions told me to wait, because they had heard that things were loosening up on the outside and Fidel was letting *Yanquis* in to look around and letting some Cubans leave. But things were so bad for us inside that I started refusing the crap they gave us to eat.

But after a week, there was a miracle. The sergeant woke us up one night and said that if we wanted to leave Cuba, there were buses waiting to take us to the port of Mariel. We all began to dance and cry and let ourselves be shoved and kicked onto the bus. The guards told us to shut up, so we rode in silence.

When we got to the port, we were pushed onto an old boat. There were too many of us, and the boat was low in the water. I was afraid it would sink, but the captain started the motor, and we traveled almost twenty hours before we reached Miami. When we got off, we all fell down and kissed the ground. I am not Catholic, but I thanked God right there.

The next months were strange and hard. I did not have a sponsor here, so I was moved from camp to camp before I got to Arkansas. [There was a refugee resettlement camp in Fort Chaffee in that state.] The people at the camp started calling us *Marielitos*, and they knew I had come from a prison. This made them suspicious, and I was interviewed six times about what my crimes had been.

I explained that I didn't have a job, and my mother was sick, so I looked in trash cans for food and slept in a doorway one night, and that's when I got arrested. None of them believed me, and they all said that no one would be sentenced to five years for such minor things. They don't know Cuba and Fidel. The other Cubans at the camp complained about the food, but I remembered what had been. *Para mi fué el paraíso.* To me it was a paradise.

After a year, someone came to claim me. My mother knew a man who had a friend who had left Cuba and was living in Houston. I had a sponsor and a job, so I left the camp in 1982.

I have been working hard. I don't understand what the rules of your country are about people like me [meaning Marielitos, rather than Afro-Cubans], but I want to stay. The only thing I have done wrong here is a traffic ticket. Oh … and I got drunk at my last birthday, but I didn't drive.

If you send me back, they will kill me. I am everything they hate—a black man without a job. I am how the revolution failed.

At the conclusion of Mr. Marcial's testimony, I sat stunned. The accounts and evidence of race-based crimes in the history of the United States are legion, but I had never heard of or even read about anything like this. In some foolish and naïve way, I had realized as a girl that blacks in my country were treated unfairly and deprived of civil rights, but I had simply assumed that when they crossed paths with particularly virulent and violent white people, the women were raped and the men were summarily hanged or shot or otherwise instantly disposed of. In other words, my concept of racial violence had heretofore been a culturally limited one.

Mr. Marcial's attorney had a few questions about the death of his mother in Cuba and about any other instances of discrimination or violence against Afro-Cubans that his client might have witnessed. Upon cross-examination, the government's attorney asked a few token questions about the possibility of escape from prison, potential job opportunities in other parts of Cuba, and Castro's assertions that discrimination based on race was outlawed. Mr. Marcial fielded these in a straightforward manner, giving as much or as little information as he had.

After both attorneys had summed up, I took a one-hour recess, formulated my decision, and returned to the bench to grant the asylum application. Mr. Marcial cried silently as I wished him well in the United States. When I got back to my office, I locked the door and cried not so silently about the great harm we cause each other because of the colors of our skin.

Reflection

It is part of an unjust society to cover up the pain of its victims.
—Dorothee Sölle

I was born in 1946 in a small town in what is called Deep East Texas, a phrase that connotes an area of the state that might as well have been antebellum Mississippi—deeply conservative though traditionally Democratic, racially segregated yet interdependent, and self-deceived in its attitudes toward what were politely referred to as "colored people." My mother grew up in that town of five thousand inhabitants, and she returned home to give birth to me with a family physician she had known all her life and to be taken care of by her own mother.

My grandmother was a forbearing and gentle woman who spoke kindly to the black people she employed, picked them up to come to work and drove them home when they were done, and continually offered to pay for any home improvements they might accept, such as electricity and indoor plumbing. She was generous with them at holidays and on special occasions, and she was lovingly cared for by them as she approached death. But she believed that "colored people" had "their place" and should know it, and she was shocked and disgusted when she once saw an interracial couple at an automat in New York City. Her reaction to them led to the only argument I ever had with her.

My grandmother's husband was an intemperate man who was said to have physically abused black people and ideologically supported the Ku Klux Klan. When I once asked my mother about this, she said that she really didn't know anything about it, but she was sure that the Klan had only been interested in "civic improvement projects."

I spent the first few months of my life in that small East Texas town being nurtured and cared for by my grandmother and her black housekeeper. During that time, my mother resumed playing bridge and having fun with her old high-school chums, and my father, who was a civil engineer, toiled away in his first postwar job as a surveyor for the Texas Highway Department. My parents soon moved to Dallas, and my mother was delighted to be living in what she thought was a sophisticated and cultured city.

After a two-year detour to Fort Belvoir in Virginia, where my father had been called back into the army to teach carpentry to soldiers during the Korean War, we returned to Dallas. I lived there until I graduated from high school in 1964, and since graduation from college in 1968, I have spent less than thirty days and nights in that city, in large part because it is a place that has always given me the racial creeps.

Texas in the 1950s and 1960s was a place of bright-line segregation, and I grew up seeing and following the directives of those signs that said Whites Only or Coloreds Only on everything: drinking fountains, restrooms, restaurants, swimming pools, lunch counters, park areas. They were probably the first things I ever learned to read. And even where there weren't any visible posted signs, the invisible social prohibitions kept schools, churches, banks, stores, and everything else strictly segregated.

Although I never discussed it with any of my childhood acquaintances, I'm sure that at least a few of them must have shared some of the confusion I felt at hearing principles of equality and the golden rule taught in our schools and religious institutions yet seeing the daily negation of those lessons in the racially divided culture that surrounded us.

My parents had bought a house in a privileged enclave located in a small city incorporated within the city of Dallas; the area was noted for the quality of its schools, and no one living outside of the district was permitted to enroll in them. I clearly recall my parents' talking about a crisis that arose when one of the residents of the enclave installed her black maid and the maid's child in servants' quarters located above the garage of her large home. Because the child lived within the exclusive school district, he had a legal right to attend the school, but some strange exception was carved out, and he was not allowed to enroll.

A more personal crisis developed for my father when, as the civil rights movement and talk of bussing gained momentum, he became convinced that our school district would eventually be integrated by the use of force and violence, and in response he began to make do-whatever-it-takes financial plans to enroll my sister and me in an all-white private girls' academy in another part of Dallas.

The extent of racial prejudice finally struck home with me as a result of two other incidents. The first occurred when a clear-thinking high-school classmate who excelled on the debate team was disciplined by the principal and ostracized by other students after she attended a local NAACP meeting during our senior year. Ordering that I have nothing to do with the girl, my mother announced that she herself was thinking of starting a local chapter of the National Association for the Advancement of White People.

The second incident was the assassination of President Kennedy on November 22, 1963—a tragedy that caused a great deal of satisfaction and relief in the area where I lived because it meant that the civil rights movement as well as Robert Kennedy's push for passage of the Civil Rights Act would probably be stalled or maybe even completely derailed. I was sixteen at the time, and it was a turning point in consciousness for me.

As I drove home from school that day, I saw a number of maids waiting for city buses on the corners of my neighborhood, and many of them were crying. I realized that, other than my grandmother, the human beings who had been the most tender and loving to me throughout my life were black people, such as maids, yard men, and my father's employees. I wondered what would happen to them now that one of their champions was dead, and I knew I could not participate in the racial status quo any longer.

As my senior year in high school began and college applications became due, my parents were insistent that I attend either a religiously sponsored university in Texas or one of the several women's colleges in Virginia. I didn't want to do either, but my preference for Smith, Radcliffe, or Sarah Lawrence was summarily ruled out, so I chose a college in Virginia. It was located on what had been a large plantation, and I found out when I got there that the charter stated it had been established for the "education of white girls and young women."

A student in my dormitory was the daughter of Asian nationals on a diplomatic posting to the United States, so the college's charter had obviously been broken. But there were no black women enrolled, and when the subject came up, most of the white Southern girls would drawlingly refer to there being other schools available for "niggras."

I was very unhappy the entire time I was there, and I eventually transferred to a school in Texas that had a student body of about six thousand, three of whom were black. One was a gifted tenor in several of the college's accomplished and well-known choirs that often made concert tours to places in and near Texas, usually staying with host families at the conclusion of every evening's performance.

At a city in Mississippi, the black choir member was not allowed to sleep in anyone's home and had to spend the night in a motel for "colored people." I was a member of the college's a cappella choir, and after our performance one night in a city in Arkansas, I was a guest in a home that had a Confederate flag prominently displayed in every room, including the bathroom. Over dinner and again at breakfast the next morning, the hosts regaled me with accounts of how integration was ruining their state and the entire South.

After I graduated from college, I spent three years in graduate school and then worked for a year as a VISTA volunteer before starting law school. In the last half of the volunteer year, I was assigned to an inner-city project in Omaha, Nebraska. I lived in a deplorable, flea-infested apartment in a poor black neighborhood and spent much of my time listening to black people tell me about their basic needs, what they wanted for their children, and what they thought politicians and the political process should do for them. I also spent time listening to them call me a honky.

When I left Omaha and entered law school, my only interests were in poverty law and criminal law, which often have unfortunate overlaps, and I was thrilled when, during my last semester, the New

York Legal Aid Society offered me a job that was to start within two weeks of graduation. By the time I moved to New York, I had lived in Texas or Virginia for twenty-eight years, and I was looking forward to being in a place where I thought racism would be minimal or nonexistent.

But even though language and terminology were different, New Yorkers practiced their own kind of racial discrimination, and as I walked the city and took in its amazing variety, I was also aware that most neighborhoods were not especially integrated and that ghettos abounded in all five boroughs. Most of my Legal Aid clients were black or Latino, and the squalor and misery in which many of them lived were not appreciably different from the living conditions of blacks and Latinos in Texas and other parts of the South.

When I finally moved back to Texas and began working as a federal prosecutor, I was stunned by the amount of racial prejudice against Latinos. I heard many colleagues and even one federal judge tell jokes about "Messicans," and I heard several social acquaintances tut-tut about the regrettable "browning" of Houston by growing Latino and Asian populations.

Even more shocking was the tutorial I received from a light-skinned black coworker about color discrimination among African-Americans themselves. According to her, the greatest prestige is enjoyed by those who are high yellow (so light as to appear to be white), followed in descending order by redbone (a mixture of white, Native American, and African); octoroons (one-eighth African ancestry); quadroons (one-quarter African ancestry); and, on the very lowest rung, those whose skin is very black and whose features are "too negroid."

Although I can no longer pinpoint the source of the information I was able to piece together at the time, the bench memo I prepared for myself in Mr. Marcial's case indicates that I had done some reading about racial discrimination in Cuba and had learned that

Afro-Cubans also have a system of social ranking among themselves based on gradations in skin color.

At the top of this pigmentocracy[11] are *blanconazos* (very white in appearance). Below them are *mestizos* and *mulatos*, who have skin color and facial features indicating racially mixed parentage. And even lower are *negros*, who have deep black skin color, negroid features, and two black parents. Thus, Mr. Marcial was at the bottom of Cuban culture in general because he was black, and he was also at the bottom of Afro-Cuban culture because he was so black (a *negro azul*). It is therefore not surprising that he was unable to find work or get prompt health care for his mother because he was so dark or that he was persecuted in prison because he was the darkest of the dark.

Mr. Marcial's asylum case was only one of a handful I heard that were based on claims of persecution on account of race. Because his was the first, it caused me to think more carefully and clearly not only about how my own behavior sometimes passively endorses racism but also about prejudices I carry in other areas. I'm not talking about a pervasive sense of white guilt over how the South bought and kept black people as slaves and freed them only after a bloody civil war. Nor am I talking about my unwitting participation in Jim Crow laws, because I was a child when they were operative in my small world. But what I *am* talking about is my occasional failure to speak out when I see injustice done because of skin color.

A few years ago as I was having dinner with some friends in a Mexican restaurant, an Anglo woman at the next table was chatting loudly with her three companions and failed to notice the busboy approach and set a glass of water at her place. As she gave a grand sweep of her arm to illustrate her story, she knocked over the glass, spilling water all over the table and into her own lap. In less than a nanosecond, her face hardened, her voice became shrill, and she began insulting the busboy in racial terms, calling him a "stupid spic who can't even serve water."

The young man spoke no English and began saying *lo siento* (I'm sorry) over and over while attempting to dab water from the hem of her skirt with a clean napkin. This enraged her even further, and she shouted for the manager and demanded that the busboy be fired for "gross incompetence" and "trying to touch my private parts." The manager addressed the busboy in Spanish, telling him to get his things and leave his uniform in his locker, and the scared teenager vanished.

Hoping to find the young man, I got up and went to the back door of the restaurant to say some conciliatory words to him, tell him that not all gringos are like that, and give him twenty dollars for ... what? Reparations? His portion of the tips that waiters were supposed to share with busboys? A sop for my own sense of shame that someone in my country would do this to a stranger?

I waited ten minutes, and when he had not appeared, I went back into the restaurant, found the manager, told him that I had seen the whole incident, and pointed out that it was not the fault of the busboy he had just fired. I asked the manager to take the kid back, but he dismissed me with "What's done is done."

As my friends and I were driving home after dinner that night, they were filled with admiration for what I had tried to do, but I was not so sanguine, for I knew that what I should have done was to confront the other diner politely but firmly at the moment the water was spilled, describe what I had seen, insist that it was an accident, and ask her to show some mercy to the frightened young busboy.

In other words, even though I had eventually taken the remedial step of trying to right a wrong, I had failed to take the radical step of engaging with the incident at its inception and addressing the injustice right then and there. I did not beat myself up over my inadequacy and ineffectiveness, but I did learn a lesson about the importance of trying to stop an act of racism before it develops its own head of steam and scalds those in its path. This requires a willingness—which I'm not sure I possess—to risk one's safety, for white supremacists and neo-Nazis continue to demonstrate that there is no fury like that of a self-righteous racist called to task for attacking someone of a different color.

What I *am* sure of, however, is that my lack of willingness is somehow tied in with what feminist scholar Peggy McIntosh calls the "invisible knapsack of white privilege" that I and other Caucasians unconsciously strap on and snack from every day,[12] and I can only hope that a continued raising of my own consciousness about active and passive racism will also raise my level of immediately available courage when I see another person being abused in any way because of color.

America is a puzzling place. The Civil War is over. Jim Crow laws are dead. The Voting Rights Act of 1965 ended almost a century of disenfranchisement of black voters that had persisted even after the Fifteenth Amendment was ratified in 1870. And we now have an African-American president.

But lawsuits seeking redress for racial discrimination still make their way slowly but successfully through the courts. The Innocence Project regularly secures the freedom of black prisoners who were wrongfully prosecuted, convicted, and sentenced by prejudiced attorneys and judges and juries and witnesses. And the flag of the Southern Confederacy can still be seen on license plate brackets and window decals, or unfurled in bars, or hung proudly in gymnasiums of public and private schools whose athletic teams use *Rebels* as their moniker, or even draped over the backyard fence of a private residence not far from where I live in this culturally diverse metropolis of almost six million people.

Obviously, then, although most of us were quick to condemn South African apartheid after we had some sense of the self-evident moral rectitude of our civil rights movement, we as Americans still have far to go in leveling the playing field of color in our own ball park.

Up until the time I heard the case of Esteban Marcial Mosqueda, I thought that the worst outcome of racism was either rape or death. The lesson of his case, however, is that there are thousands of ways to kill the inner life of a man or a woman because of his or her skin color. And although the victims of race-based torture and degradation may physically live beyond the crimes committed upon them, the scars on their bodies and minds will last forever and will stand as constant reminders of how our own revolution as individuals, countries, and a world community continues to fail.

This is a hard lesson for me to take in, but it is nevertheless a blessing, for it has further opened my eyes about what I need to do to stir my own life out of passivity and into advocacy for the strangers we continue to create and maintain in our own midst.

As the fourteenth-century Persian poet Hafiz wrote, "All the hemispheres in existence lie beside an equator in your heart."[13] If I and we can't get beneath the latitudes of color that lie on top of us, how can we ever get to the equator of our common heart?

2. Persecution on Account of Religion: Josué Maldonado Ortiz of El Salvador

Background

Like many civil wars throughout history, the one fought in El Salvador from 1980 to 1992 was rooted in the obscenely unequal distribution of wealth within that small country. Since the latter part of the nineteenth century, El Salvador's major income-producing crop has been coffee, with all of the labor being done by peasants and most of the profits being reaped by the country's small percentage of wealthy citizens.

As far back as 1932, socialists had attempted to organize and lead poor people and indigenous populations in uprisings against the government, and the government had consistently responded with killings carried out by its military death squads. Over the next four and a half decades, the military and its opponents (guerrillas) engaged in frequent skirmishes, several assassinations and coups, and constant infighting within each group.

In 1979, a military junta overthrew the government and pledged various reforms. When it became apparent that these promises would not be kept, the guerrilla groups united to form the Farabundo Martí National Liberation Front (FMLN), named after an early leader who had been arrested and put to death by the military. The civil war

23

began in earnest in March 1980 when Archbishop Oscar Romero, an outspoken advocate for the poor, was assassinated while saying mass at a small chapel within a hospital.

During the next twelve years, the government-supported military and its death squads targeted anyone who was suspected of supporting social and economic reform, including but not limited to clergy, union members, intellectuals, and students. And, of course, the peasants themselves were tortured and killed, their homes shot up, and their crops burned.

The violence of government security forces received international attention when they raped and murdered four American church workers in 1980 and when they shot to death six Jesuit priests, their housekeeper, and her daughter at night in 1989.

Meanwhile, the FMLN and its members blew up bridges, destroyed coffee plantations, cut power lines, and generally tried to bring down the economy upon which the government and military continued to operate. The guerrillas also murdered and kidnapped military, government, and public officials and their families.

From the early days of the war, the United States supported the Salvadoran military government and wanted the American public to believe that the guerrillas were part of a socialist conspiracy posing an imminent threat to this country. In a televised address on May 9, 1984, President Ronald Reagan stated that "San Salvador [the capital of El Salvador] is closer to Houston, Texas than Houston is to Washington, D.C. Central America *is* America. It's at our doorstep, and it's become a stage for a bold attempt by the Soviet Union, Cuba, and Nicaragua to install Communism by force throughout the hemisphere."[14]

As the United States continued to supply the Salvadoran government with millions of dollars and hundreds of military advisors, scant concern was shown for the growing body of information about the activities of the death squads and their violations of human rights. Several Salvadoran presidents were elected in the 1980s, but each proved ineffective at restoring order, controlling the military, or leading the country to the successful conclusion of peace talks that were begun more than once but that fell apart each time.

Finally, in 1990, after El Salvador had essentially cannibalized itself and lost at least 75,000 of its citizens to the murders and assassinations carried out by both sides, the United Nations intervened, and sustainable peace talks began.

In 1991, the military and the FMLN signed a peace agreement in New York. In 1992, the Peace Accords of El Salvador were signed in Mexico. Later that year, the United Nations began an investigation of human rights violations, and it also found that the military was not complying with the peace accords.

The United States ended its military aid to El Salvador in 1990, but in 2000 it managed to persuade the government there to let it set up a military base at the national airport in San Salvador, purportedly to combat drug trafficking.

In Court

I went on the bench one Tuesday morning in 1988 and attended to several routine matters, such as continuances, motions, and pleadings, before Josué Maldonado Ortiz's case was called for his asylum hearing. Because no attorney had filed a notice of appearance during the six months in which the case had been pending, I correctly assumed that Mr. Maldonado would be representing himself, and I had therefore allotted only two hours for the hearing, thinking that it would go rather quickly.

In my review of the asylum application the previous afternoon, I had noted that the claim was based on religious persecution, but there was no information in the application itself about any facts that would support the claim. Most of the cases I had heard from El Salvador in the preceding year had been based on harm and mistreatment and persecution because of political opinion, so my interest was piqued by something a bit different even though I didn't yet have much to go on.

Because immigration courts that are located in nondetained settings do not have bailiffs, the interpreter went to the waiting room and escorted Mr. Maldonado to a counsel table about ten feet in front of the bench and across the center aisle from the table used by the INS attorney.

According to his asylum application, Josué Maldonado was thirty years old, but like many people who have lived the rigors of poverty, he looked much older. He was dressed in a clean but frayed long-sleeved white shirt, and I could see the bulging outline of a small book in his thin left breast pocket. He also had on heavy dark green cotton pants, which led me to guess that he worked for a local landscaping company, and on his feet were vinyl lace-up shoes that looked new and did not fit him properly. He was tall and lean and very tan, and he carried a wide-brimmed straw hat in both hands.

I introduced myself and the interpreter and asked Mr. Maldonado to be seated. As it often happened with people in court, he was overly deferential, gave an awkward half bow, and said, *"Buenos días, Señora Jueza."* Good morning, Mrs. Judge.

The previous day I had heard a different kind of case from an African country that was formerly part of the British Empire, and the respondent in that case had variously addressed me as Madam, Your Lordship, My Lady, and finally Your Worship. I had begged him to just call me Judge or Your Honor, but his nerves had prevented him from settling on either one, and if his claim had not been so serious, the entire proceeding would have been comical. So on this particular Tuesday morning, I was more than willing to be called Mrs. Judge.

I asked Mr. Maldonado to approach the witness stand and raise his right hand to be sworn. But I realized immediately that if he was a religious man, he might want to affirm instead of swear, and I therefore asked him which he preferred to do. He opted for affirming that the testimony he was about to give, as well as the information in his asylum application, was the truth, and he then seated himself in the witness box.

As was my practice with pro se respondents, I began by marking the application itself as Exhibit #1, verifying what little biographical information there was in it, and making notes on my legal pad about other things that should have been included but had been omitted—siblings, parents, any relatives in the United States, kind of work the respondent had done in El Salvador, date he had entered the United States illegally. The investigative summary offered by the government's attorney stated that Mr. Maldonado had come to the attention of the INS during a "workplace sweep" (a raid) of a local car wash business.

Generally, legal procedure in American courtrooms favors testimony to be adduced in question-and-answer format, and when it isn't, it is common for the opposing side's attorney to interject, "Objection. Narrative." When dealing with respondents having little formal education and no familiarity with being rigorously interrogated in a courtroom, I usually overruled such objections by the INS attorney, choosing instead to ask the respondent for a narrative that, if it got too far afield, could always be reined in and brought back to questions and answers.

Turning to Mr. Maldonado, I said, "Your asylum application says that you were persecuted near your hometown of El Mozote [a small and remote village in the Department of Morazán in northeastern El Salvador] because of your religion. Tell me as many things as you can remember about what happened—the date, the weather, the time of day, even what you were wearing, and who it was who harmed you and exactly what they did."

For the next three hours, I sat next to Josué Maldonado and listened to his quiet voice tell me in simple language the following:

On the fifth day of September in 1984, I was working in the fields behind my family's house. I lived with my mother and father and three younger brothers. We are *campesinos* [peasants who work the land], and we grow rice and beans and vegetables to eat and to sell to our neighbors. There is always something to do to take care of the crops.

My mother and father and brothers attend the Catholic church in our town. I was baptized and prayed and went to mass for many years there, but sometime about five years ago a friend of mine went to San Salvador to work, and when he came back, he was Pentecostal and no longer Catholic.

Day after day he talked to me and told me it was much happier to be Pentecostal, and after many months I went with him to the house where he prayed. He was right! People there were singing and moving and reaching their hands up to God, and they prayed for themselves. No one needed a priest anymore!

I felt good in my heart when I left, and I kept going back until I said I wanted to be part of them. They gathered around me and touched me and said *bienvenidos* [welcome], and I felt young again. They even gave me a small Bible to carry in my pocket. I read a little—no big words—but having my pocket filled with God gave me protection. When I told my mother and my father what I had done, they cried, but I am the oldest son, and they needed me.

On that day in September it was hot, and I was bending down to pick some beans before they rotted on the ground. When I looked up, I saw some men coming across the field toward me. I am a little—what do you say, where I can't see

28

very far? [Here, I asked the interpreter to use the Spanish word for *near-sighted,* and Mr. Maldonado agreed that was what he meant to say.] They were moving fast, and when they got near me, I saw they had guns. I was not too afraid, because the war was going on and many people carried guns. I quit having one when I became Pentecostal.

Then they were standing right in front of me, and when I saw they were wearing unmarked uniforms [no stripes or insignia], my fear began. I had heard about *los escuadrones de la muerte* [the death squads], and I was praying that they had not come for me. They were loud and smelled like beer, and after they shot some bullets over my head and into the air, they started pushing me and grabbing at my clothes.

I had my Bible in my shirt, and when it fell out on the ground, they laughed and cursed and said they had some plans for me. I thought of my mother and father, and I got on my knees to beg for my life. But the soldiers pulled me to my feet, opened my Bible, and started reading the story of the crucifixion of Jesus to me. I had many tears, and I knew I would be killed.

What happened next is hard for me to say to you. The soldiers ordered me to take off my clothes. I started with my shoes, and then my shirt, and then my pants, and then my underwear. After I was naked, they pushed me back and forth between themselves, hit me in my chest and back with fists, and banged my legs with their rifle butts. All the while, they told me that it was *pobrecitos* [poor souls] like me who were ruining the country with stupid religion and its ideas and that they wanted to baptize me in a toilet.

But there was no toilet nearby, so the soldiers baptized me with their urine. After that, they made me stand naked in the field, and as they pressed the muzzles of their rifles on my throat, they tore my Bible apart and made me eat it page by page.

It was almost dark before they finally went their way, and when they left they took my clothes. I lay on the ground to rest for a while, and when it was night I went back to my family's house.

My mother took care of my bruises, and I think one of my knees was broken. She sent for my friend from church—the one I told you about who had been to San Salvador—and he came to my house to pray for me. I told him about my Bible, and he gave me his. He said that everyone involved in the war did things like this to people of my church and that I would be better off leaving because now they knew who I was and where I lived and what I believed. He gave me some money, and I hid it for two months until my knee was stronger. I left El Mozote one night, and now I am here.

Yo creo yo creo yo creo mi jueza, la luz del mundo es Cristo. I believe, I believe, I believe, my judge, the light of the world is Christ. I cannot give up my faith, even after what happened. It gives me joy, and makes me better, and lets me talk to God when I am working in the fields. I walked through Guatemala and Mexico to get here, and I am praying you will let me stay where I can have my Bible with me every day.

When Josué Maldonado had finished speaking, the courtroom was silent for several minutes, and I fought for my own composure. Eventually, I turned to the INS attorney and asked her if she wanted to cross-examine the respondent, and when she said yes, I explained to Mr. Maldonado that the government's attorney would be asking him some questions.

In any private or public-sector law office, there will always be varying degrees of ability among the lawyers vis-à-vis certain skills of the trade. Some attorneys excel at writing briefs but are tongue-tied at trial. Among trial attorneys, some seem to excel at direct examination or opening statements, whereas the forte of others might be cross-examination or summation. Sadly, some attorneys excel at nothing, and so it was in the case at bar.

I wanted to believe that the INS attorney, whom I knew to be a devoutly religious person, was as convinced by Josué Maldonado's testimony as I was. And I was hoping that she would simply waive cross-examination, which was usually a signal that the INS would not oppose a summary grant of asylum, thereby relieving me of the necessity of giving a lengthy oral decision from the bench or taking the matter under advisement and later rendering a lengthy written decision.

She elected, however, to launch into a meandering cross-examination that seemed to suggest that if there was one shack or shanty in El Salvador where Mr. Maldonado could hide and read his Bible, the persecution he experienced was not countrywide, the claim was therefore groundless, and the application should not be granted.

During the twelve years I practiced law, I was the beneficiary of excellent and rigorous training courses in trial and appellate skills offered by the three public-sector offices for which I worked. Many attorneys, however, begin their careers as solo practitioners and soon find that they have little time or money to spend on training seminars and practicums that would improve their performance. As far as I could tell, most of the training the INS gave its attorneys was in-house and was understandably focused on the complex nuances of the law itself rather than on courtroom skills.

In the course of the hour in which the INS attorney tried to shake Mr. Maldonado's account of his shaming in the field and the sincerity of his belief, he kept his hand over the Bible in his shirt pocket (and thus over his heart) and remained steady. When the attorney finally announced that she had no further questions, I told Mr. Maldonado he could step down and take his seat at the counsel table.

I then informed the attorney that I intended to grant the asylum application, and I asked whether she would accept that decision and waive appeal or whether she wanted an oral or written decision from which to take an appeal. She requested a short break to confer with her supervisor, and while she did so, Mr. Maldonado and the interpreter and I sat in the courtroom in silence. The attorney returned within five minutes and informed me that the government would accept my decision and would not appeal.

Granting asylum to a person is an experience like no other, and it is much like saying, "I hereby spare your life." Not once in eighteen years did it fail to move me in the deepest part of my soul, and not once did any applicant hear the granting words and fail to weep with relief and gratitude.

Josué Maldonado cried like a child and buried his face in his Bible. I went back to my chambers, cried uncontrollably, buried my face in the holy book I kept there, and knew that this was the case that had broken me open forever.

Reflection

Blessed are the meek, for they will inherit the earth …
Blessed are those who are persecuted because of righteousness,
for theirs is the kingdom of heaven.
—Mathew 5:5, 10

Of the many reasons for which people persecute each other—and of the five specifically mentioned in American asylum law—perhaps the hardest for me to understand is persecution based on religion.

Race and social groups are easy markers of otherness, and they trigger their own kinds of apprehensions and revulsions. Nationality incites feelings of xenophobia as well as fears about boundaries and containment and encroachment. And political opinions breed inflammatory rhetoric, false promises, and concerns about who wants to take what from whom or deny what to whom.

But religion is such a matter of the heart and soul, and it seems especially inhuman and inhumane to try to destroy another person because of what he or she believes about what is transcendent, unseen, and unprovable. Or maybe this is the very crux of what is so fear-inducing—the fact that, ultimately, belief is not factual or visible or audible but merely felt, and is therefore an enormous threat to those who chart their courses by the coordinates of philosophical materialism.

I have thought of Josué Maldonado Ortiz many times since I heard his case twenty-five years ago, and each time I choke up because the memory touches something deep in me. I have never been able to articulate exactly what that something is, but I know that when my voice catches and my tears start, some blessing has usually been received in my own soul.

Initially, I know I am moved by his attraction to the simplicity of the faith he adopted after experiencing its joy. I and most of the people I know have grown up in complicated religions and denominations that call for elaborate rituals, ceremonial artifacts and attire, dietary restrictions, formulaic prayers, theological verities, and prescriptions and proscriptions and commandments that, as my friend Bruce says, ultimately weave a funeral shroud around what should be a joyous life.

This same friend is a staunch supporter of guidelines and even rules promoting civility and respect and tolerance and peace, and he is also fond of saying, "Sometimes we feel guilty because we *are* guilty." When Bruce's conscience pains him, he is thoughtful and serious about what is causing it, and he is quick to seek forgiveness and make amends when he believes he has wronged another person. When he concludes that his only offense has been against God, he is equally quick to ask for forgiveness, and he believes that God will provide an appropriate avenue of corrective action to which he (Bruce) has a responsibility to stay open.

The net result of this rather stripped-down and decent way of being in the world is that Bruce, who has a PhD in physics, lives a simple life, has loyal friends, enjoys nature, journals his dreams, e-mails his grandchildren every day, means it when he says he is happy, and is as clear as a bell emotionally. He keeps abreast of opportunities for learning and improving his soul, believes in following good light wherever it may lead,[15] occasionally attends a church or a synagogue when he hears of a sermon or program that might enrich his understanding of what constitutes right thinking and right action, periodically takes courses at the local Jung Center to keep his right brain stimulated, and does not drag around a ball and chain of guilt.

Bruce stays current with himself and is, as someone once described the singer Joan Baez, "utterly without guile." And although he wouldn't dream of keeping kosher or fasting on Yom Kippur, there is something about the single-minded and unencumbered ethic of Bruce's life that always makes me think of him as a prime example of someone who is living Jewishly.

About two years ago, I attended an informal Saturday evening concert of folk music featuring Small Potatoes, a husband and wife who sing wonderfully together and who are also talented songwriters and instrumentalists. I was unfamiliar with most of what they sang, but all of it was pleasant, tuneful, reflective, socially conscious, and often funny.

Near the end of the concert, the wife laid down her hand drum and said that the next song would be sung by her and her husband while he played the guitar and she signed the words in American Sign Language. What followed was a beautiful rendering of "Simple Faith," written by David Tamulevich of the duo Mustard's Retreat.[16] This was another song I had never heard, but I thought of Josué Maldonado Ortiz as it was being sung, and I realized at the end that I was not the only person deeply affected by it. I come back often to the words and the message of the song and especially to the chorus, which reminds me so much of a man who suffered because of what he believed:

> Ours is a simple faith,
> Life is a short embrace,
> Heaven is in this place ... every day.
> Hope is the ground we till,
> Make each day what you will,
> Thankful for dreams fulfilled ... every day.

There are other aspects of Mr. Maldonado's story that have become metaphorical for me and, in so doing, have raised questions and taught lessons, as many metaphors will do. I am using the concept of metaphor here rather loosely,[17] but the first is that of God—or whatever name we want to give to that which we think of as transcendent—as one who covers us, and the second is that of God as one who feeds us. If we want to think of the metaphors playfully (and there is certainly no sacrilege or disrespect in doing that), we can refer to them as God the clothier and God the chef.

I like interesting acronyms and was delighted a number of years ago when a Unitarian minister told me that G-O-D stands for "good orderly direction." I hear many New Age people refer to this concept as The Universe, and I have also heard several others of the same persuasion refer to it as Spirit or as Divine Intelligence. A friend of many years refers to it as Whomst, and I have recently seen God referred to in theological writings as The Holy and Wholly One and as All That Is.[18]

I frequently follow the Jewish practice of not saying God's name outside of a liturgical context and instead use *HaShem,* meaning "the Name." And I am always stopped short by wonder and mystery when I enter a synagogue and see inscribed over the Ark containing the Torah scrolls the Talmudic directive (in transliterated Hebrew), *Da Lifnei Mi Ata Omed.* Know before whom you stand.

None of the names for God matter, of course, especially to those who truly believe in something greater than themselves, and we busy ourselves with verbal expressions of faith and with some good works to prove our beliefs. But few of us give much thought to how (or if) we bare ourselves before this greater being or what discomfort the exposure gives us when we do.

It is one thing to confess our sins and seek forgiveness or absolution or whatever it takes to offload the misery of guilt. But it is quite another—at least for me—to give words to all the ambivalence and ambiguity and paradox that struggle within me when I try to acknowledge the darker parts of myself, or to know and admit that I am holding something back when I say that I trust HaShem to guide me and care for me, or to own up to how human and small and petty and flawed I feel so much of the time.

The irony in all this humiliation caused by my limited undressing of myself before God is that God presumably already knows where all the warts are and, as with Adam and Eve, will kindly assume the role of the Great Seamstress and give me something with which to cover my nakedness.[19] Still, I continue to work on going spiritually *au naturel* before the Holy One, and I probably would not ever have done so in the first place without the image of Mr. Maldonado before me.

The other metaphor I have extrapolated from his story is that of ingesting holiness, and I have tried to imagine how my life might be changed by a complete taking in of faith. As I listened carefully to Mr. Maldonado's testimony and sensed his absolute credibility about the events he described, I realized that he had made no effort to protest or stop the meal of Bible pages he was being made to eat, nor did he mention choking on them or having any adverse physical consequences from what he was forced to do. The fact that he had rifle muzzles pressed against his throat did not seem to be the operative factor in the seeming ease with which he stood naked for hours and ate his holy book, and I was left with the strong impression that he felt he was honoring God by enduring what was necessary to stand up for his faith.

I have no concept of what it means to totally immerse myself in the study and practice of holiness, and although I spend two hours every morning reading soul-provoking books, I cannot fairly say that I ingest or absorb them, nor can I say that I would sacrifice my life or my dignity for them or the teachings they contain.

I do know, however, that for people of faith, there are gunpoint moments and events when we are required to choose what (if any) received wisdom we will internalize and whether we will stand for something or for nothing, even if we don't know exactly before whom we stand. And I also know that the best and most memorable conversations I have ever had, whether with friends or with strangers, are those in which one or some or all of us have been talking about what is sacred to us. We may not be using the word *sacred* as we speak, but that is still what the topic is, and the passion and energy and connections of the exchange are exhilarating.

One of the most interesting things about our minds is how associative they can be. For example, the first name of a New York friend of mine is Joseph. When I heard of him before I met him many years ago, I immediately thought of the biblical Joseph, who was an interpreter of dreams. The New York Joseph went to law school and became an attorney at the urging of his parents. A few years after graduation, however, he decided to follow his passion, and he went back to school and earned a doctorate in clinical psychology. He now mostly works with children, and he likes to tell me that I am the only person who is not surprised that he has authored several papers about their dreams.

Similarly, when I first met Mr. Maldonado, my mind turned to the name Joshua (the English version of Josué) and to the biblical story of the conquest of Jericho. Although I initially saw no parallels between Mr. Maldonado and the mythic proportions of the historical Joshua, I decided on a whim to reread the story in the Hebrew Bible.

The account begins immediately after the death of Moses, when God appoints Joshua to lead the Israelites across the Jordan River into the land that God has promised them. In his appointment instructions, God tells Joshua, "Be strong and resolute; do not be terrified or dismayed, for the Lord your God is with you wherever you go" (Joshua 1:9).[20] Upon reading these words, I could think of no better description of the way in which the Salvadoran Josué withstood what members of the death squad did to him, and I have often wondered if he knew the story of the biblical hero whose namesake he was.

From that mental association, I next began remembering a brief visit I once made to the city of Jericho, and this in turn prompted me to recall the phrase Jericho Road, which entered our language from the New Testament parable of the Good Samaritan and has become a metaphor for a time of lonely hardship or suffering.

As recounted in the Gospel of Luke, the parable was told by Jesus in response to a Jewish legal scholar who was trying to bait him with questions about eternal life, loving God and one's neighbor, and who exactly is one's neighbor. According to the parable, a man was traveling on the road from Jerusalem to Jericho when he was attacked by robbers who stripped him of his clothes, beat him, and left him half-dead by the side of the road, and it was not until after two pious Jews passed him by on the other side that he was eventually rescued and cared for by a compassionate lower-class Samaritan.[21]

And so my loosely associative Josué-Joshua-Jericho mental loop came into focus and encircled the gentle man who sat beside me in court many years ago. For as he encountered his attackers and stood naked in the field of beans and rice that became his own Jericho Road, Josué Maldonado Ortiz knew what was sacred to him because he had found joy and comfort in an uncomplicated faith that taught him to reach upward with his hands to a strong and present God, to speak directly to the Holy One, and to carry wisdom in a pocket next to his heart.

I still choke up every time I think of him, but I now understand that the abiding blessings of his life on mine have been the vision of a simpler faith than the one I had been trying to practice, the knowledge that what is sacred is always close by, and the lesson that the ingestion of holiness requires a kind of nakedness and courage that I do not have but pray to someday learn when I am working barefoot in the field of my own soul.

3. Persecution on Account of Nationality: Khalid Talhami of Palestine

Background

In the late nineteenth century, Jews in Russia were terrorized, persecuted, and murdered during the anti-Semitic pogroms carried out by the country's monarchy and its agents. Understandably, a large number of Russian Jews decided to leave their homeland, and over the next fifty years many departed for Europe and the United States. A substantial number, however, decided to resettle in Palestine and reclaim what they believed to be their ancestral birthright to the land of Abraham, Isaac, and Jacob and the kingdoms of David and Solomon, and they began doing so in the early 1880s, often referring to themselves as *Hovevei Zion*, Lovers of Zion.

Although early Zionist leaders, such as Theodor Herzl and Chaim Weizmann, had originally considered first Argentina and then Uganda as potential locations for a Jewish homeland, those possibilities were eventually jettisoned in favor of Jewish settlement in Palestine.

As Zionists arrived in Palestine, which was still part of the declining Ottoman Empire, they began buying up land individually, continued making purchases through the Jewish National Fund after it was founded in 1901, and started establishing Jewish communities in what had been a predominantly Arab and Islamic region for more than twelve centuries. Much of the land obtained by Jewish settlers was bought from absentee Ottoman landlords who had no reservations about selling their property to incoming Zionists. What is especially noteworthy is that most of these transactions were carried out without notice to or concern about the Palestinians who lived on and worked the land.

As it became clear that Jewish colonists intended to have far more than small enclaves of culture, safety, prosperity, and religious freedom for themselves, and in fact appeared to be determined to dispossess the majority Arab population of as much land as possible, native Palestinians began to protest, for many of them were *fellahin* (peasants) whose existence and livelihood depended on what they obtained from the plots of land they had been renting from wealthy Ottoman landholders. Additionally, Zionists encountered opposition from Bedouin shepherds who feared that the new Jewish settlements might affect their nomadic movements or the grazing habits of their livestock.

From 1882 to 1917, there were a number of sporadic clashes between Palestinian Arabs and Jewish settlers, but a more organized Arab resistance was also forming and being expressed in meetings, leaflets, newspaper articles, and petitions to the Ottoman authorities.

In 1917, with no foundation or authority whatsoever in international law, the British government stepped into the growing conflict and issued the Balfour Declaration, which announced Great Britain's support of a Jewish "national home" in Palestine and its intention to assist in the formation of such. Although the document seemed to promise the Arab population continued civil and religious rights, Palestinians and other Arabs were quick to notice and argue that the declaration was essentially a British promise to the Jews of a land that was not Britain's to dispose of. Many historians have subsequently attributed the solidifying of Arab resistance toward

Zionism—as well as antipathy toward Jews—to the Balfour Declaration.

Near the end of World War I, British forces defeated Turkish forces in Palestine in 1918, and the entire region came under British administration via a mandate drafted by the victorious Allies and eventually approved by the League of Nations. Two states, Palestine and Transjordan, were established under the mandate. Great Britain administered Palestine on behalf of the League of Nations from 1920 until shortly before Israel declared statehood in 1948. With the aid of extralegal Jewish paramilitary groups, the British heavy-handedly quelled all attempts by indigenous Palestinians to revolt against the strictures of the mandate.

During World War II, the British further tightened their control of the area by restricting Jewish immigration into Palestine, and at the conclusion of the war, they prevented thousands of Holocaust survivors from entering, diverting many of them to internment camps in Cyprus and even returning some of them to Germany. These actions angered militant Jews living in the area and prompted Jewish paramilitary organizations to initiate armed attacks against British forces.

By the end of 1945, Great Britain's war-shattered economy could scarcely afford the cost of maintaining troops in Palestine, and public opinion had also turned against the British because of their immigration policies about Jews.

In a sharply divided vote in November 1947, the United Nations General Assembly approved a plan to partition the area of the British mandate (Palestine) into separate Arab and Jewish states. Zionist leaders welcomed and accepted the plan, but Palestinian leaders and other Arab and Muslim countries in the region rejected it. Civil war immediately broke out, and within five months Jewish forces had prevailed, but not before hundreds of thousands of Palestinians had fled or been driven out of their homeland.

On May 14, 1948, Israel declared itself an independent state, and temporary borders (the Green Line) were established. Jordan annexed the mandate's regions of Judea and Samaria (now known as the West Bank), and Egypt gained control of the Gaza Strip in the south. Neither Jordan nor Egypt gave much attention to the statelessness of the Palestinian refugees within their territories, and no Palestinian Arab state was ever founded.

In the more than six decades of its existence, Israel has been beset on all sides by Arab nations and their allies who believe that it has no right to exist and that the Jews should be driven into the sea. Attacks against Israel and its cities and citizens have ranged from large-scale terrorist activities (such as car bombs, airplane hijackings, and the mass murder of Olympic athletes) carried out by Arab groups based in surrounding countries, to more widespread conflicts and provocations that led to the 1967 Six-Day War (launched by Israel against Egypt, Jordan, Syria, and Iraq), the 1973 Yom Kippur War (initiated against Israel by a coalition of Arab states led by Egypt and Syria), and Israel's 1982 invasion of Lebanon after a militant splinter group of the Palestine Liberation Organization (PLO) attempted to assassinate the Israeli ambassador to the United Kingdom.

From its inception, however, Israel has been far from blameless and has rested the case for its existence on questionable arguments that Jews have an exclusive historical right to the land and that a Jewish state is necessary not only to correct two thousand years of injustice but also to prevent further persecution.

When faced with isolated attacks by small guerrilla groups, Israel has frequently responded with air raids and commando operations, and when confronted with street mischief, such as the throwing of stones at Israeli soldiers, the armed forces have retaliated with incursions into civilian homes and properties that have often appeared to be far beyond proportion to the original damage inflicted.

When Israel has been successful in taking Palestinian land beyond its borders, it has often been reluctant to enter into ceasefires or other agreements that would involve giving back any of those areas. In the 1967 war, Israel captured the West Bank, East Jerusalem, the Gaza Strip, the Sinai Peninsula, and the Golan Heights. Israel eventually incorporated the Golan Heights and East Jerusalem into its sovereign territory and gave the inhabitants there permanent residency and the opportunity to apply for Israeli citizenship.

Israel returned the Sinai Peninsula to Egypt in 1982, and it claims to have completely disengaged from the Gaza Strip in 2005, although it retains control of airspace and coastline in the area and is still viewed as an occupying power there by the United Nations, by Palestinians, and by a number of countries and human rights organizations.

The West Bank, which is by far the largest piece of formerly Palestinian land in the area, remains under military occupation, and the residents there are not permitted to become citizens. The United Nations regards the West Bank, East Jerusalem, the Gaza Strip, and the Golan Heights as "the Occupied Territories" because of the degree of control Israel exerts over each. Israel prefers the term "disputed territories."

International law governing military occupation generally requires an occupying power to maintain the status quo until the signing of a peace treaty or the formation of a new civilian government. Israel has chosen to ignore that obligation by encouraging and financially subsidizing Jewish settlements in the occupied territories, legalizing ones built without authorization, selectively protecting the settlers in their disputes with the Palestinians upon whom they are encroaching, and systematically harassing and detaining Arab citizens of the occupied territories who have no history of militancy, terrorism, or anti-Israel activities.

Because of these perceived violations of international law, as well as dependency on Arab oil interests, many nations have severed diplomatic relations with Israel, which, save for its ties to many American Jews and the billions of dollars it receives yearly in aid from the United States, is becoming increasingly isolated in the world community. Since 1969, the United Nations has demanded the right of self-determination for Palestinians and has repeatedly condemned Israel's occupation of Arab territories, the disproportionate ferocity of many of its reprisals, and its practices as an occupying power.

In 1993, Israel and the PLO signed the Oslo Accord, an agreement that established the Palestinian Authority as a five-year interim administrative organization to govern parts of the West Bank and the Gaza Strip. Now, twenty years later, the status of the Authority is still nebulous, it is by and large toothless, and it serves as a constant reminder that the Palestinians' hope for national sovereignty remains a distant one.

All attempts at peace negotiations between Israel and the Palestinians have either fallen apart completely or become hopelessly deadlocked, and repeated Palestinian appeals to the United Nations for recognition as an independent and autonomous state have been met with opposition from Israel and the United States.

More than a century and a quarter after Zionists first began arriving, Palestinians have no country to call their own, and most of them who still live in what was once their homeland do so in fear of and at the mercy of the occupying forces of Israel.

In Court

Khalid Talhami first appeared before me in 1994. At the time, he was clean-shaven and was wearing a suit and tie. I explained that the United States government was seeking to deport him because he had overstayed the visitor's visa he had obtained in Jordan. I advised him of his rights, and because he had no criminal record, I offered him the opportunity to admit to the charge of deportability and to accept what was called voluntary departure, whereby he would agree to leave the United States within ninety days at his own expense. By doing this, he would avoid having a deportation order on his immigration record should he wish to return to this country in the future. Mr. Talhami politely but firmly declined my offer, and he requested time to get an attorney.

When he returned to court three months later with a lawyer, I asked for pleadings. The attorney admitted that Mr. Talhami was not a citizen or a national of the United States and that he had indeed stayed longer than his visitor's visa permitted. He denied, however, that his client was a native and citizen of Jordan, and he stated that Mr. Talhami was a Palestinian who would be seeking asylum because he had been abused by the Israeli army.

These pleadings put the case in a temporary limbo: I could not allow the respondent to file an asylum application without a determination of his nationality, and the United States did not recognize Palestine as a nation. Thus, I made a finding for practical purposes that Mr. Talhami was "a native and de facto citizen of what is now called Israel," and I set dates both for the filing of an asylum application and for the hearing itself.

On the day of the asylum hearing on a Friday morning in 1995, Mr. Talhami appeared in court wearing a traditional *thawb* (a long cotton tunic) and sandals, and he was carrying a Ziploc bag containing a black and white patterned *keffiyeh* (a large square of cloth draped to form a head covering). He had also grown a short beard that made him look older than his thirty-two years.

I invited everyone to be seated, but Mr. Talhami's attorney asked to approach the bench. When I motioned for him and the government's attorney to step forward, the lawyer started babbling whispered apologies for Mr. Talhami's attire and insisting that he had instructed his client not to dress that way for court. I told the attorney that as long as people were modestly dressed, I didn't care what they wore to court, and I asked him to return to his seat so we could begin the hearing.

When I had received the properly filed asylum application some months earlier, I had seen that it contained only one claim: that Mr. Talhami had been used as a human shield by the Israeli army on at least a dozen occasions in his native city of Hebron, which is the largest city in the West Bank and is located about nineteen miles south of Jerusalem. Hebron is holy to Jews because it is thought to be the burial site of the patriarchs Abraham, Isaac, and Jacob as well as the matriarchs Rebecca, Sarah, and Leah, and it is also holy to Muslims because of its association with Abraham.

In my initial review of the supporting documentation attached to the application, I had immediately identified one issue on which I wished to receive pretrial briefs by the parties and a second matter about which I wanted to consider their opinions before the start of the hearing. The first issue was whether using noncombatants as shields was a violation of the Geneva Conventions, which I thought it surely must be, and the second was whether either attorney or Mr. Talhami himself thought I should recuse myself because I am a Jew.

Both parties had submitted timely briefs about the first issue, although neither was especially well-written or helpful. And as everyone sat in front of me on the day of the hearing, I asked about the second issue. The government's attorney made a few obsequious remarks about how he thought I would do a fine job in the case no matter what my "personal proclivities" were, and Mr. Talhami's attorney stated that he had conferred at length with his client, who was of the opinion that Jewish judges in America could be trusted to be fair. I then addressed Mr. Talhami directly through the Arabic-language interpreter and asked if he wanted me to recuse myself because of my faith, and he said no.

I have never understood the traditional oath, "Do you solemnly swear to tell the truth, the whole truth, and nothing but the truth, so help you God?" It has always seemed like so much legal verbiage, and from the first case I ever heard, I opted to use the following: "Do you swear or affirm that the testimony you will give today and the information contained in your asylum application are the truth?" With a reply in the affirmative from Mr. Talhami, we began.

My name is Khalid Talhami. I was born in Hebron in Palestine in 1963, and I lived there all my life. My father sells many things in the bazaar—small paintings, perfumes, prayer rugs, pottery, postcards of the tombs, and some bracelets and rings. It varies all the time, but he is honest, and customers always find him.

We are not poor or rich. I finished school, and before I left my country I had a good job tutoring young boys in Qur'an at the mosque. The imam trusts me, and teaching satisfies me.

I did not often leave my city, but six years ago my uncle in Jerusalem got sick. My father himself was not well, and since I am his oldest son, he asked me to go and visit his brother to see if he needed help from my family, especially since the month of Ramadan was getting near. I packed a few things and thought I would be back in two days. I also borrowed a friend's car. Mine was getting old and needed repairs.

There are Jewish settlers in Hebron, and they make life hard for us. They think they own the place. The army watches out for them and lets them bother us and then always blames us for the trouble.

As I was leaving to see my uncle, I had to go through a checkpoint with the soldiers less than a mile from my father's house. My father had told me to have my identity card out of my pocket so they could see it quickly, and I gave it over out the window with my left hand. [Here, Mr. Talhami held up his hand, showing that half of his index finger was missing.]

The lieutenant saw my finger and asked me what had happened. I told him that I had lost part of it when I was about fifteen. I was at a friend's house, and we were playing with his older brother's electric saw. I was foolish and careless, and my finger went through the blade.

The soldier said, "You can't prove that, and I know what really happened. You were playing with explosives, and that means you are a terrorist who wants to kill Jews. You have lied to me, and now you will have to pay." The soldier opened the door and pulled me out of the car. He called the others over and told them I was a demolition expert, and they started to talk about how I could be of use to them. They spoke Hebrew very poorly, and I knew they were not *sabras* [Jews born in Israel]. They took down my name and address, tied my hands in front of me, and said they wanted to give me a new job that very day.

Soon, another car drove up. Inside was a Muslim family. The soldiers made them all get out, and when they saw that one of the women was with child, they told me to raise her dress so they could be sure the baby was not really a bomb. She and I were both in shame from this. After that, they made me lie on the ground and crawl underneath the car looking for explosives. They had already used their mirrors on poles and knew there weren't any.

The soldiers kept me at the checkpoint until night and then released me to go home. They said there was no way they were going to let me go to Jerusalem. I went back to my father's house, and when I told him what had happened, his dark skin turned pale.

Several days later, I was getting ready to go to the mosque and teach. When I opened the front door of my home, two soldiers were standing on the outside. They said, "It is time for you to go to work." They put me in a truck, and I knew they were not taking me to my students.

I rode with them to an old Palestinian neighborhood not far from a Jewish settlement. After they tied my hands, they told me they were going to search many homes looking for weapons, and I was going to be their insurance that nothing would happen to them. I asked to call the imam so my students would not worry, but they said I had more important work to do.

All morning they pushed me ahead of them as they went house to house looking for any forbidden thing. They never knocked, and they scared many women and children and old ones. They would just go in, touch whatever they wanted, open cupboards, take fruit, and leave with anything they said was suspicious, such as a small knife. In one house, they even sat down and watched TV for a while.

When they left me at my father's house that afternoon, I knew nothing would remain the same. I was marked. I told my father what had happened when he returned from the market in the evening, and I saw such anger and sadness in his eyes.

Over the next many months, the soldiers would appear whenever they chose and would take me with them, and it was always the same. We would go to a Palestinian neighborhood, they would start making a lot of noise, people would come to the windows and see me in front of the soldiers, and they would not shoot. When we went into the houses, the soldiers would put a rifle in my back and tell me to get down like a dog and sniff for explosives. I was frightened every time. After several months, I started keeping a secret list of all the days it happened.

Because my father is an honorable man, he knew many people to call and pay. An old family friend lived in Jordan and knew someone who worked for the government there. I don't know how much it cost, but my father got a passport for me along with a visitor's visa for the United States. I was told to say that I was entering the United States for the wedding of a cousin in Houston. I have no cousin in Houston, but I was carefully coached about him and his bride and how our families are related, and I was told that someone by that name would back me up if I got stopped.

I was able to get to the airport in Amman, and from there I went to Rome and then Amsterdam, where I got a flight to Houston. By the time we landed, I had practiced my story for over eighteen hours, and I passed immigration with only a few questions. After I got my suitcase, I saw my name on a sign being held by someone in the airport. I went with him and was taken to the house of a man from my country who was married to an American woman.

I have been here six years. I know that my visa was for six months only and that I was not allowed to work. But I could not go back, and I could not be idle.

I have worked some as a tutor at a mosque in your city, and I have also worked at a gas station. I think one of the customers there turned me in to the immigration authorities. Several agents in green uniforms came one day to buy fuel and candy bars, and they asked to see my identity documents. I showed them my passport with the expired visa, and they arrested me right away. I was taken to a detention facility, but at least they did not make me crawl and search for explosives.

I know you are a Jew, and you probably feel much about Israel. But I did no wrong. If I return, I have no place to go except my father's house. The army has a long memory, and I will be used by them again.

I live with the knowledge that by asking you to save my life, I will never see my family again. So much is unclear. I leave it in your hands.

After Mr. Talhami finished his narrative, I asked the INS attorney whether he had any cross-examination, and he said yes. What followed was a disorganized and desultory inquiry into Mr. Talhami's attitude toward Judaism (irrelevant), his knowledge about bomb-making (nothing), and the reasons Palestinians think they are entitled to their own country (indicating the attorney's lack of background reading and preparation for the hearing). I asked the attorney to address the issue of the Geneva Conventions, and he replied, "Aw, Judge, this is just a minor American courtroom, and it really doesn't matter here."

I was about thirty-five when it dawned on me that one could hardly beat the synergistic benefits of experience and perspective, especially when it came to the practice of law and the living of life. By the time I heard Mr. Talhami's case, I had been in the legal business for about twenty years and on the bench for almost eight of them, and I had seen a broad range of attorney skills and behaviors on display.

For several years when I worked in New York, I thought the practice of law was done in a pretty sophisticated way until one day when I was waiting to argue a pretrial motion in Manhattan Supreme Court (which, contrary to its name, is the trial court of general jurisdiction in the state of New York and the equivalent of a district court in Texas). There were more than two hundred cases on the docket, and mine was number 187, so I sat back to enjoy the pageant and the hubbub.

At some point, the bailiff yelled out the name of a case, and an attorney about my age went skidding up to the podium, giving a loud "whoa" as he came to a halt. When the judge asked him why he had not filed a written opposition to the defendant's motion to dismiss, the attorney gave an all-over body shimmy and announced in his best imitation of one of comedian Steve Martin's *Saturday Night Live* routines, "I forgot!" As the judge stared at him, the attorney started laughing uncontrollably and finally managed to choke out, "Holy shit, Judge, where's your sense of humor?" Without missing a beat, the judge said, "Motion to dismiss granted. Next."

By this time, the attorney was almost paralyzed with laughter, and the immediate scenario ended when the bailiff took the young man's arm and led him out a side door. I don't know what came over me, but I was filled with compassion for this lawyer who was obviously unraveling on the spot, and I went to find him to see if he was all right. I spotted him buying a tabloid at a newsstand inside the building, and I approached him and asked if anything was wrong, fully expecting to find that he was intoxicated or perhaps high on cocaine. But he seemed unusually calm and sober as he told me that he just could not take the pretentiousness of if all anymore.

My mind flashed back to this incident as I looked at the government's attorney in Mr. Talhami's case and wondered if his stated opinion about the unimportance of the proceedings and of the Geneva Conventions was the first sign of a similar professional meltdown that would later lead to some unfortunate and embarrassing incident in court.

I took a breath and reminded him that even though we were certainly not the Supreme Court or even the federal district court, we were willing participants in a process set up by law to determine the extent of harm to real live human beings and whether they could stay in this country with us, and that it was my habit in all such cases to consider every international humanitarian law to which the United States was a signatory.

The attorney gave a loud and dramatic sigh and said, "Yeah, well, okay. As best I can make of the Geneva Conventions, you're not supposed to use someone as a shield, and since it looks like you're gonna grant the case anyway, I don't have anything more to say." I told him that I would take his remarks as a waiver of further cross-examination and of summation, and I then asked Mr. Talhami's lawyer to sum up, which he did with unnecessary bombast as well as references to matters not in evidence, each of which I struck from the record even though I heard no objection to them from the INS attorney.

Because the facts of the case had not been complicated, I was ready to issue an oral decision from the bench and did so immediately, finding that the way Mr. Talhami had been treated by the Israeli Defense Forces (which some Israelis refer to as "the most moral army in the world") was an aggregate of sustained psychological harm and abuse constituting persecution, that it had been inflicted on him because of his Palestinian nationality, and that he had therefore sustained his burden of proving his eligibility for asylum.

Mr. Talhami had learned quite a bit of English during his six years in the United States, and he understood the outcome of his case even before I asked the interpreter to explain it to him in Arabic. I saw his eyes fill with tears, and he raised his right fist to the upper area of his left chest.

On many occasions as an adult, I have been the beneficiary of Muslim hospitality, and even though a courtroom is not a place of social greeting between a judge and a litigant, I nevertheless heard myself speaking the few Arabic words I know to Mr. Talhami: "As-salaamu alayka. Peace be upon you." Mr. Talhami was briefly surprised but then bowed slightly as he replied, *"Wa'alayki salaam.* Peace also with you." And to this I responded, *"Insha'Allah.* God willing."

Mr. Talhami then turned to his attorney, exchanged a quick but full embrace, and began walking toward the back door of the courtroom. I saw him remove his keffiyeh from its plastic bag and start to put it on his head, and since the time was around noon, I knew he was headed to his mosque to pray to the same God I would be addressing in synagogue services later that evening.

Reflection

If a stranger lives with you in your land, do not molest him.
You must count him as one of your countrymen and love him as yourself,
for you were once strangers yourselves in Egypt.
—Leviticus 19:33–34

In 1975 my ego succumbed to flattery about my leftist politics, and I accepted an invitation to join a feminist-Marxist study group in New York composed mostly of women faculty and graduate students at Columbia University. We met on Wednesday nights in one of those shabby West 115th Street apartments that belonged to the university and were inhabited by scholars who were as indifferent to their surroundings as they were preoccupied with causes and ideas. Dutifully, I and the other twelve group members trudged through *Das Kapital* and debated at length about what does or does not constitute use value and labor value.

One evening, during our strictly observed twenty-minute break for the holy trinity of coffee, chocolate, and cigarettes, I happened to mention having recently attended a meeting of Shalom Achshav (Peace Now), an organization dedicated to bringing an end to the seemingly never-ending conflicts between Israel and its Arab neighbors.

Twelve very bright Jewish heads immediately swiveled approvingly toward me, and slogans began flying like shrapnel: "Zionism is racism!" "Zionism is colonialism!" "Zionism is imperialism!" Karl Marx was forgotten, and for the next two months we became an ad hoc feminist Jewish talking group with thirteen different views about Israel and the Palestinians. The only things we agreed on were that we were all offended to some degree or another by Marx's having written about "the woman question" when there was no question in our minds, and that we would therefore not refer to our current discussions as having to do with "the Palestinian question."

My own rather reductive position was this: Zionism was not a bad idea in theory, but in practice and execution it has been a disaster because it has resulted in the subjugation and displacement and impoverishment of those whose lands we took. A few members of the group agreed with me, but several told me that I had no standing to advance this position because none of my own family members had been imprisoned or had perished in pogroms or in the Holocaust. This is true, but it is also true that the household in which I grew up was a dangerous place that could not honestly be called a home by any semantic stretch, and the country in which I grew up could not accurately be described as homey to homosexuals and other groups outside the white, heterosexual mainstream.

And so even though I have no known ancestors who were always looking over their shoulders to see if the Cossacks or the Gestapo were coming, I do have some personal knowledge of what it is to long for a home where I could be safe and for a homeland that delivers on its pledges of liberty and justice for all. Of course, I did not share these observations with the other women lest I be thought of as having fallen into the trap of believing that the personal is the political, which all of us in the group would have surely denounced as bourgeois thinking at its most deplorable.

By some echolocation, we Jews seem to find each other, and when stereotypical looks and surnames don't clearly identify us, it is usually some properly pronounced or inflected Yiddish word that sets our radar beeping. "Are you Jewish? Yes? Oh, thank God." And we almost invariably seem to lapse, either consciously or not, into some groupthink that makes us huddle together, shift into a *shtetl* (small village) mentality, and begin to talk in terms of Jews and *goyim* (gentiles), us and them.

Shortly after my feminist-Marxist study group began talking about Zionism, I went with my friend Devorah to visit her elderly mother at the Jewish Home for the Aged in the Bronx. I had never met her mother and knew nothing about her except that she, like Devorah, had struggled long and hard with depression. Miriam Greenberg greeted her daughter warmly and me almost as warmly, asking me right away if I was Jewish. When I replied, *"Nu,* sure," she began speaking to me in Yiddish. My insubstantial knowledge of German, Russian, and Hebrew let me follow along a bit, and I responded in English sentences punctuated by any Yiddish words and phrases I knew.

The three of us had a pleasant visit for about an hour until it was time for Miriam to go inside for dinner. As Devorah and I helped her up by her elbows, the sleeve of Miriam's oversized sweater slid backward, and I saw the numbers tattooed on the inside of her forearm. My stomach turned over, and I had a visceral understanding of the impulse behind Zionism.

About two weeks later as I was sitting in the back of a courtroom in Manhattan waiting for my client's case to be called, a young man wearing a yarmulke was brought in before the judge. He was in handcuffs, had a black eye, and was being arraigned on an assault charge. The judge shouted at me ("You from Legal Aid back there") to approach and take the case, and thus began my representation of Dov Aronoff, a sixteen-year-old member of the Jewish Defense League who had used his carefully honed karate skills on a dark-skinned subway passenger after a pro-Israel rally at the United Nations.

According to Dov, the other man was speaking Arabic and making fun of Dov's yarmulke and *peyos* (earlocks). As it turned out, the victim of Dov's assault was an Indonesian national who had been speaking Javanese while pointing at a map behind where Dov was sitting on the Lexington Avenue IRT and who had suffered a serious injury as a result of Dov's Bruce Lee–style flying kick to the head.

In a small interview room, my client spoke passionately about the necessity for the Jewish Defense League, and when his father came to bring him a kosher hot dog from the Second Avenue Deli and to post his bail, the father broke out in a cold sweat and fainted in the waiting room. When I reported this to Dov, he said, "Yeah, he and his family were taken before some Nazi court when he was a kid, and he has never gotten over it." Again, Zionism made sense to me.

Of the five asylum cases contained in this book and the hundreds of others I heard over the years, perhaps none ever presented me with more irony, paradox, and inner turmoil than this one.

I have recently talked about each of the cases with a discerning listener, and when she finished hearing about Khalid Talhami, her response pointed me to the initial irony: unlike the other four, "there was not a scratch on him," she said. Yet the Israeli army had systematically whittled away whatever tenuous sense of safety and security he might have had as a resident of an occupied territory so that by the time he left his homeland, he had suffered a soul death from which he may never recover. Indeed, he had been completely stripped of his dignity and his peace of mind, and the new covering with which he chose to clothe himself was a fierce and saturating hatred for Jews.

Other ironies and paradoxes arose as the case got underway. At a synagogue social event about a year earlier, one of the Jewish law partners of Mr. Talhami's Jewish attorney had told me that the firm's informal motto was "Never trust the fucking Arabs," so I was initially caught up in some misgivings about another Jew. I wondered why the lawyer in court with me had taken the case of someone from a group he categorically distrusted, and I also mentally questioned whether he would be or could be the best advocate for Mr. Talhami.

Additionally, the Arabic-language interpreter who had been hired for court that day was a perfectly trilingual Jew who had grown up in Palestine and later immigrated to the United States after being educated in Europe and marrying an American citizen. I sensed some tension between him and Mr. Talhami from their first exchange, and I was uneasy about whether I was getting a completely accurate translation.

The remaining ironies and paradoxes could best be summed up in this way: I was yet another Jew deciding the fate of yet another Palestinian, and I felt off-balance and miserable.

In one of his many fine poems, twentieth-century German playwright and theater director Bertolt Brecht wrote, "So many reports. / So many questions."[22] There are indeed many reports, many hard questions, and no easy answers about what has happened and what continues to happen between Israel and its Arab neighbors, although it seems important for me to periodically remind myself that this is not so much a conflict between Jews and Muslims, whose Abrahamic religions and precepts are so similar, as it is a geopolitical impasse over who has the right to live on a piece of land that includes a city deemed holy by three major religions.

But notwithstanding the lack of facile explanations or answers or solutions, it is equally important for me to remind myself that hard questions can be not only spiritual gifts in themselves but also are, in fact, the stuff of Judaism: our bottom-line methodology is dialectic, and we have a way of self-criticism that has generally driven our thinking forward and placed us in the thick of, if not at the front of, so many just and right causes, such as the civil rights and feminist movements.

I am not a spokesperson for Judaism, and I have never resided in Israel, so I can talk only about my lived experience of this faith tradition and about my belief in the imperative of a safe haven for Jews. But I have many questions about Israel's policies and practices toward the Palestinians, and my first one is, How did we go from centuries of victimhood at the hands of Catholics and Protestants, and from being the targets of Tsarist Russia and countless other kinds of governments and regimes, to being the oppressors and abusers of Palestinians? It seems that many of us have lapsed into what psychologists call destructive entitlement—the belief that we have been wronged, that we therefore deserve something, and that we have the right to take freely from the Palestinians as a salve for the wounds that repressive governments inflicted upon us.[23]

I also wonder what would have happened if, instead of buying pieces of Palestine without notice to and regard for those who were depending on the land for their lives and livelihood, we had simply and publicly asked the Ottomans or another country to sell or give us a certain amount of land to establish a safe place for Jews. And what would *we* have thought and felt and done if the situation had been reversed and Arabs had begun surreptitiously buying up land upon which we had lived and worked and depended for survival as the majority population for twelve centuries? And how similar is our treatment of Palestinians to what was doled out to Native Americans by European colonists and settlers?

Have we labeled Palestinian and Arab resistance to our actions as anti-Semitism and countered that with our own form of racism? And even if some Jewish acquisition of Palestinian land has been legal, has it been moral and ethical? And can we really call any place our homeland if it exists because of our exploitation of others? And have we forgotten that being chosen people does not mean being chosen for privileges but rather for the responsibility of having a positive, light-giving effect on the larger world? And are Israel's official policies and actions toward Palestinians perversions of Judaism? And do we have the courage to undertake a radical analysis of the roots of this state of perpetual conflict and saber rattling and to acknowledge our own past and present wrongdoings? And finally, are we so lacking in confidence about our own training in *din* and *rachamim*—justice and mercy—that we cannot believe in and work for a two-state solution that would bring an enduring peace to this place we want to call home?[24]

What further troubles me about all this is the sad irony that in our desire to create a place of permanent safety and refuge for any Jew who wishes to avail himself or herself of it, we have built a nation that is perpetually at ideological war within itself and at physical war on its borders.

Although none of us would expect each other to give up our dialectical method or the millions of questions we ask each other as Jews every day, it is disheartening to know that debate within the State of Israel rages continuously and acrimoniously about who is a Jew, whose level of observance is more devout than whose, and whether women should be allowed to pray at the Western Wall. And as for the physical aspect, Israel seems to me to be one of the more unsafe places in which to travel or live, with border and checkpoint and settlement skirmishes almost every day, and wars or armed conflicts always on the horizon. I have not been in Israel since 1963, and although I often think of returning for a visit of one or two weeks, I cannot bring myself to do so as long as the country continues as an occupying force with the attendant dangers that has fostered.

A friend recently asked me if I was leaving Judaism, and I replied, "Not entirely, but I think Judaism is leaving me." As I have aged, I have come to cherish the rituals of candles and wine and challah on Friday nights, a day of rest and reading and prayer on Shabbat, contemplative practices like Mussar study and its development of a soul curriculum, praying outdoors every morning while wrapped in my *tallit*, and the peaceful meditation and chanting that are increasingly being engaged in by innovative Jews seeking to deepen their spirituality.

But yes, I do see that I am leaving things like Shabbat services that are handed over to representatives of groups selling Israel bonds. And I am also leaving those boards and organizations and adult education classes where voicing support for Palestinians or questioning the rectitude of Israel's policies and practices draws icy stares and silence. In other words, I am leaving those places where I believe that the container of Israel has eclipsed the content of Judaism, and where identity politics and a reflexive attitude of "Israel, right or wrong" have overshadowed our radical requirements to do justice and love the stranger.

"Two Jews, three opinions" is a frequently heard saying in the Jewish community. A recent report from Israel's Central Bureau of Statistics estimated that the worldwide Jewish population is almost 13.5 million, so there currently must be around twenty million opinions about Zionism and Israel among those who are Jews. In the past one hundred years, those opinions have divided congregations, ended friendships, and even destroyed some families, and I am cognizant that the writing of these words may cause serious disruptions in my relationships both with other Jews and with many Christian friends and acquaintances whose support of Israel is absolute and unquestioning.

The existence of Israel is a fact that does not disturb me, for I cannot change history, but the continued mistreatment of

Palestinians feels like a black hole in the moral universe that we as Jews purport to inhabit and uphold. It gives me some relief from despair that many individual Jews and Jewish organizations both within and outside of Israel share these thoughts and views and are actively seeking redress for Palestinians. And I hope there is truth in Dr. Martin Luther King Jr.'s observation that "the arc of the moral universe is long, but it bends toward justice."[25]

I don't know when bumper stickers first started appearing on vehicles, but over the years I have variously found them to be amusing, repulsive, and thought-provoking. In the third category, I have especially appreciated these: "Live simply, so others may simply live," "The best things in life aren't things," and "God bless the whole world. No exceptions." But my all-time favorite is one I saw in the early 1970s before the war in Vietnam ended, and it was this: "If you want peace, work for justice." That has stayed with me, and I think its wisdom is applicable to every conflicted personal or political situation that I know of or have ever been involved in, including but not limited to any negotiations between Israel and the Palestinians.

I am a Jew who believes that there is much to be learned from the literature of other faiths, and my morning readings recently brought me to these words by Joan Chittister, a sister in the Roman Catholic Order of Saint Benedict:

> The brink of conflict brings us all, nations as well individuals … to reexamine our best beliefs and our most pernicious responses to them. What kind of country, what kind of person do I really want to be? And is this really the way to become it? … The way we handle conflict brings us face-to-face with ourselves. It is we who are being tested for character in conflict, not the enemy, not the other. Confrontation, to be successful, righteous, holy, must be

based on respect for the other. We are brought to learn in conflict that we are not the masters of the universe ... When the only resolution of a conflict is the complete humiliation or destruction of the other, we have long abandoned righteousness in favor of unmitigated power. But for conflict that leads to justice for both sides, sing alleluia loudly. It is the beginning of the reign of God.[26]

I hope that a reexamination of our beliefs about and our responses to Palestinians will lead the State of Israel and all Jews to a God-reigning peace illuminated by respect and justice for both sides.

The blessing for me of Khalid Talhami's case was one in disguise, and it did not reveal itself to me for several years. But the essence of the blessing was its unsettling not only of me and my assumptions about Israel but also of my unexamined loyalty to a country we Jews long to call our spiritual home. When I began preparing for this asylum hearing, I quickly realized how little I actually knew about the founding of Israel and how much I had relied on other people's rhetoric and ideas (and even a Hollywood movie) in forming my own.

In getting ready to give Mr. Talhami his day in court, I spent more time in pretrial reading and thinking than I had in any case before it or in any case that followed it. And I became painfully aware of how even the subtlest form of violence, such as buying land without regard for the people who depend on it for their lives, can only spawn more violence.

In the process of trying to work his job, love his family, and live his life, Khalid Talhami was used a shield by Jewish soldiers who had not lived on the land as long as he and his family had. It is one of the lasting satisfactions of my time on the bench that I was able to offer him a shield in return.

4. Persecution on Account of Membership in a Particular Social Group: Elena Segura Jiménez of Nicaragua

Background

Civil war in Nicaragua began in July 1979 when the socialist Sandinista National Liberation Front overthrew the dictatorship of Anastasio Somoza Debayle. Almost immediately, groups opposing the Sandinistas' revolution began to form, re-form, merge, separate, shift allegiances and ideologies, and divide. By and large, these groups consisted of those who had supported the Somoza regime (including the military), those who had supported the Sandinistas but had become disillusioned with them, and those who had not been involved in the revolution but had grown to dislike the authoritarianism and the socialism of the Sandinistas.

These opposition groups were popularly referred to as *Contras,* meaning counterrevolutionaries, and they waged a bloody and often disorganized war against the new socialist regime until the Sandinistas were turned out of office in 1990 with the presumably free and fair election of Violeta Chamorro, who was the candidate of a prodemocratic opposition party.

During the first six years of the eleven-year civil war, the Contras not only committed horrendous human rights violations but also received massive financial and military backing from the United States, notwithstanding knowledge on the part of the Reagan administration about murders, rapes, tortures, kidnappings, arsons, and destructions of property that the Contras committed against civilians (including some children).

In 1985, however, and for reasons not primarily having to do with human rights abuses, Congress cut off all funds for the Contras. What followed were secret efforts by the Reagan administration to obtain continued funding and military supplies for the Contras from private sources and through other countries, culminating in the Iran-Contra affair disclosed in 1987. This scandal revealed that money for the Contras had been procured through arms sales by the United States to Iran, all deftly orchestrated by Oliver North with the aid of the Central Intelligence Agency.

Amnesty International and other human rights organizations have thoroughly documented the violence and abuses of the Contras, with most of those reports characterizing the atrocities as prevalent, systematic, indiscriminate, consistent, terroristic, brutal, and deliberate.

By the end of the war in 1990, approximately 60,000 Nicaraguans had been killed by one side or the other.

In Court

Elena Segura Jiménez wore the darkest black to court when she appeared for her asylum hearing in July 1989. No doubt someone had told her that her words would carry much more weight if she was all in black and not in colors that the village women of her country usually wear. I too was all in black, with perspiration forming underneath my cotton-polyester robe, and both the INS attorney and the court's interpreter were wearing stylish black suits.

Miss Segura was accompanied by a male cousin who had lived in the United States for four years, and he was dressed in black pants and a black shirt.

The atmosphere seemed somber and funereal, and I paused briefly before I gave the oath and informed this small and frightened twenty-two-year-old woman that if her cousin was to be a witness in her case, he would have to remain in the waiting area until it was his turn to testify. This requirement is often referred to as the witness exclusion rule, and it is designed to prevent witnesses from hearing each other's testimony or conferring with each other and thereby collectively meshing their stories into one conforming account. Miss Segura could not understand this, and when I asked the cousin to leave the courtroom, she began to cry.

The asylum application Miss Segura had submitted to the court eight months earlier was typically sparse and had no supporting documentation, but it did note that she had been apprehended by the INS while working illegally as a "salad girl" at a downtown restaurant. She had managed to list relatives already in the United States, but none were from her immediate family.

The application also stated that she had been persecuted in Nicaragua because of her race, but she did not appear to be of any indigenous group I was familiar with or to have any African heritage, so I was a bit puzzled about what I usually thought of as the nub of the case. I went over the biographical data with her and then asked her who had prepared the application. She told me that she had paid a hundred dollars to a *notario* to do it, and I realized that we would be starting the case from the ground up.

Although I'm sure some of them mean well, notarios in Houston are generally notaries public who have paid a fee to the state of Texas to obtain a permit and an embossing stamp so they can set up shop verifying identities and signatures. Many of them have a desk within the office of an *abogado* (attorney) in Latino neighborhoods, and many of them feel free to illegally dispense legal advice, most of which is incorrect. In many Latin American countries, notarios are government functionaries who are authorized to conduct arbitration and mediation and render judicial decisions and who therefore have a certain prestige. So it is no surprise that many people who enter the United States illegally and soon find themselves in deportation proceedings turn with misplaced hope and trust to local notaries for help in facing government processes here.

I explained to Miss Segura that her Houston notario had checked the box marked "race" as the reason she was applying for asylum, and I asked her if any member of her family had dark skin or was of Indian heritage. She was visibly surprised by what I was saying and told me that her problem in Nicaragua was "because of an attack." After I instructed her to tell me what had happened in as much detail as she could remember, she began:

> I am Elena Segura Jiménez. I am from Tisma, a *pueblo* [small town or settlement] near Masaya [a city about twenty miles southeast of Managua]. I lived there all my life, and I have grandparents, aunts and uncles, and many cousins in that place. My father died five years ago, and my six brothers watched for me and worked and made us laugh at night. I took in laundry with my mother, and all of us were happy in the house.
>
> On the tenth day of April in 1987, I had taken all the laundry to the customers and was walking home along a path with trees. I heard a noise, and when I turned around, a group of men—I counted six—were walking near my back and pointing at my hair. At first I thought it was a *turba* [a marauding gang, usually composed of young men], but they looked too old for boyish pranks. I don't know much about the war, but I wondered if these men were part of it.

At first it seemed they meant no harm and only wanted to flirt. I kept walking, but I talked to them when they spoke to me, and I offered them water as we got near my house. They said yes with smiles and winks, and I went inside while they waited in the tiny courtyard in the back. I came out with a jar and cups and poured some water for them all. They laughed and talked, told me I was pretty, and asked about my husband. I said I was not married yet, and then they asked if I had brothers. I gave their names, and when the men asked more, I told them where my brothers worked. That was the last thing I said that day.

They said, "We are Contras, and we haven't had a woman in a week." The one who was the leader made a sign, and all the others circled me and started tearing off my clothes. I had on a white blouse and a red skirt with yellow flowers. I had never been with a man before, and I was very afraid. [At this point, I stopped Miss Segura and asked her if she would like to continue her testimony with the assistance of a female interpreter instead of the male who was working with me in court that day. She replied, "No. I am finally talking," so we continued as we were.]

The six forced me to the ground, and their leader took first turn. He squeezed and bit my breasts, and then he entered me with such great force I thought I would be torn apart. The pain was great, and he was large, but he finished soon. I felt my blood down there and only wanted to get up and clean myself. But then the other five took their turns. They too were quick, but here I lost my mind. [When I asked her to clarify this, she said, "I went another place inside," which I understood to mean that she mentally dissociated from the brutality. I asked Miss Segura to tell me anything else she could remember about the incident, and she continued.]

Este fué el momento en que los mangos maduros. This was the time when the mangoes were ripening. I could see them hanging large and full above my head, and I could smell their sweetness in the air. It is something you don't have here. I miss it so much.

After that, the men turned me over, and all six of them, starting with their leader, took me from the back. [Again I asked for clarification, this time inquiring whether she was referring to vaginal or anal intercourse, and she indicated the latter. At the time of this asylum hearing, there was no firm precedent holding that women are a particular social group. If this had been just a "regular" gang rape, prevailing law would have viewed it as a common street crime rather than as persecution. But if instead it had been an attack motivated not only by power but also by a desire to punish and humiliate the victim, it would have come within—or at least closer to—the ambit of established asylum criteria.]

When they had all finished, they zipped their pants, wrapped my clothes around my face and head, and called me *puta* [whore] as they left. I felt so dead. I lay there in the courtyard on the coolness of the stones. They soothed my breasts. When I got up, my blood was everywhere. I wanted to wash myself, but the men had taken the water jug with them, and we had no more left at home that day.

I tried to dress myself but could not make the buttons fit. When my mother found me, she cried so hard. She took me to a clinic in the town, and the people there washed me and gave me pills to make me sleep. I stayed three days, until I could walk again.

My brothers went in search of the men who had done this to me but did not find them. It took them several months, but finally they got the money to send me here. I stay with my aunt and her son. I want to go home. I miss *mi mamá*. I have lost my heart. I can have no children. No man will want me.

Ayúdame por favor, ayúdame. Help me, please help me.

At the end of her testimony, Miss Segura was weeping silently. I asked her if she wanted her cousin to testify for her, explaining that it would only be helpful if he had witnessed the attack on her or if he had firsthand knowledge about how the Contras treated women. She said that he had been gone from Nicaragua for many years and had not seen anything while he was there, so I told her that I would decide her case on her testimony alone.

The INS attorney waived cross-examination of Miss Segura but asked to make a closing argument. Unlike many immigration judges, I permitted and encouraged closing arguments, for I believed that they were sometimes helpful to me in getting a bigger picture or in clarifying the point of view of each side. In criminal proceedings, the prosecution customarily has the right to make the final closing argument, and since in my own previous work as an attorney I was familiar with that format, I applied it in the courtroom where I sat. I gave Miss Segura the opportunity to tell me anything else about her case she wanted me to know, but she had nothing more.

The government's attorney then began summing up. He characterized the gang rape and sodomy of Miss Segura as "an unfortunate mugging by some sexually deprived thugs," insisted that women are not a particular social group, and concluded by stating that the wreckage of Miss Segura's life could be viewed as merely collateral damage in a civil war and certainly not as a basis for granting asylum.

Equanimity is a quality much to be desired in a judge in any forum. After listening to the government's summation, I did not lose mine, but I felt a kind of anger unfamiliar to me. I told the attorney that I was not going to address either the strange sociology behind his bald assertion that 51 percent of the world's population is not a particular social group or the thinking (if any) behind his use of the words *collateral damage*. But I *was* going to say, as one former government attorney to a current one, that this is not the kind of argument that federal appellate courts (which are composed solely of attorneys who now work for the government as judges) want to see from someone who is on the same payroll as they are.

As the words came out of my mouth, I realized that I was probably sounding as crass and small and self-righteous as the closing argument I had just heard, and I made myself stop and declare a twenty-minute recess.

When I returned to the bench, I asked the interpreter to escort Miss Segura and her cousin in from the waiting room, where they had been clinging to each other during the recess. I had them sit at the counsel table together as I gave a lengthy oral decision finding that women are indeed a particular social group and that the rape and sodomy of Miss Segura had been perpetrated on her precisely because she was a member of that group.

Because oral decisions from the bench can be as complicated as written decisions and often involve many citations to authoritative cases, it was my practice not to have the interpreter translate the decisions while I gave them but instead to wait until I was finished and then tell the asylum applicant what my decision had been and the reasons for it. I verified that the INS attorney reserved the right to appeal my decision (although he never took an appeal), and I then told Miss Segura that I was granting her application for asylum. She had not stopped crying since her testimony began three hours earlier, but her tears and sobs were now obviously those of relief, as were those of her cousin, and she began saying *gracias* as if it were a mantra.

I always felt protective toward unrepresented respondents, and if there was any helpful information I could offer them at the end of a hearing, I did so, such as the importance of applying for lawful permanent residence within a year of the asylum grant and then applying for US citizenship within five years of obtaining permanent residency. Although it would have been improper for me to make referrals to private individuals for posthearing services, I had no qualms about letting Miss Segura know about counseling available to rape survivors at a nonprofit area women's center.

As with all people to whom I granted asylum, I took the opportunity to wish them well in this country, and I even learned to say it in Spanish for those whose language it was: *Bienvenidos a los Estados Unidos. Espero que usted y su familia encuentren la paz y la prosperidad en este país.* Welcome to the United States. I hope you and your family find peace and prosperity in this country.

It has been my ongoing hope for the past twenty-four years that Elena Segura Jiménez has indeed found peace in my country.

Reflection

We realize how frail a word is when faced with the thing it names.
—Julia Alvarez

I was sixteen years old in the summer of 1963 before my senior year in high school, and for reasons that are not important here, my parents determined that I would spend six of the twelve precious vacation-from-school weeks traveling through Europe and the Middle East with one of their friends who was organizing a tour. I did not want to go, but I really had no choice in the matter.

In Syria, during a day trip to excavated ruins near Palmyra, I tripped and fell while trying to step over a large pile of stones. The layout of the site had necessitated our group's proceeding in single file with one nimble guide in front and another with a club foot bringing up the rear, and I was at the back of the group. As the ones ahead of me turned a corner and moved out of my line of vision, the rear guide came up behind me, telling me in broken English to wait so he could help me.

He then pulled me roughly to my feet and began grabbing my breasts, reaching under my skirt, and trying to kiss me on my face and neck. Even at just five feet five inches and one hundred pounds, I was still much larger and stronger than he was, and I managed to fight him off and run toward my group, which had not missed me at all. I reported the attack to the group leader (my parents' friend), but he took no action except to make a mild verbal complaint to the guide who had been in front.

In the many years since then, I have been the target of sexually motivated assaults on three other occasions. One was by a drunken date when I was in college, and I managed to avoid being raped solely because I was sober and therefore quicker.

In 1974, while attending a party for a friend who was in one of my law school classes, her physician husband followed me into the powder room of their home, locked the door behind him, and tried to rape me, all the while demanding that I describe to him in graphic and vulgar detail how excited he thought I must be getting. He and I were about the same height, and it was only by a fluke of leverage that I was able to pull him off balance and escape.

The last assault was on a Friday night in 1977 as I was walking out of a New York gay and lesbian synagogue in the West Village where services had just ended. A man sprang out at me from a narrow space between two brownstones, screamed that I was "a dyke and kike" who was going to "get the real thing," and pushed me to the pavement. By then, I had been running thirty miles a week for several years and had also been taking karate and self-defense lessons, so I was able to get up quickly, stomp hard on the arch of his right foot, slam the heel of my hand upward under the bottom of his nose, and run away.

In 1983, I was working on Sunday afternoons at a women's bookstore owned by a friend of mine and located on the Upper West Side of Manhattan. My primary duty was to stock new arrivals, and I always looked forward to opening the carton Karyn had left for me, breathing in the smell of new books, and going through them slowly while sipping the strong Dominican coffee I had bought at a nearby bodega before reporting for work.

On one December afternoon, the first book out of the carton was *Places in the World a Woman Could Walk*, with the front of the dust cover noting that it contained stories by the talented American writer Janet Kauffman.[27] When I saw the title, the only word that formed in my brain was *nowhere,* and I set the book aside, erroneously thinking that it was probably a collection of short stories about women who had been the victims of violence.

My involvement in feminism began in 1970. Of all the issues it has raised and the changes it has engendered, the one most important to me has been the safety and integrity of women's bodies, whether considered in terms of freedom in reproductive matters or freedom from physical and sexual harm. Throughout my years of ongoing education and concern about this topic, I have never forgotten that I am living the privileged life of a white, middle-class American and that millions of other women living in this same country have suffered physical and sexual violence on a level that completely overshadows the four assaults I was able to fend off.

I have listened as the victims have spoken and written of incest, rape, and sexual abuse, and for several years my practice as a licensed massage therapist was limited to women who had suffered greatly from those acts of violence. But nothing prepared me for what I heard from so-called Third World women as they testified before me about atrocities that had been committed on their bodies and about the habitual unwillingness of the authorities in their countries to receive the victims' complaints, to pursue the perpetrators, or to treat the crimes as anything other than a man's right to do whatever he desired with a woman.

Elena Segura Jiménez was one of many women who sought asylum based on sexual crimes against them by strangers. There were others, however, who sought protection in the United States because of domestic violence, and it was not until 2009 that regulations and decisional law began to consider those assaults as something more than private crimes and therefore within the purview of asylum eligibility.

Equally horrific have been the asylum cases of many African and Middle Eastern women detailing practices coyly referred to as FGM, a sanitized acronym for female genital mutilation, which is in turn a sanitized umbrella term for clitoridectomy and infibulation. In the former, a woman's clitoris and often also her labia minora are removed either by slicing or snipping; in the latter, the sides of her vaginal opening are sewn together. Both atrocities are performed without anesthetics, both are designed to prevent the girl or woman from having sexual pleasure, and in addition to the unspeakable psychic trauma of the mutilation, each often results in sepsis that sometimes leads to death or to lifelong genitourinary problems, pain, and disease.

Every person on earth experiences what philosophers call an existential loneliness occasioned by the fact that no one, no matter how attuned he or she might be to another person, can ever see life through the other person's lens. Because each of us possesses our own unique history and assemblage of events and emotions, all of which are filtered by what we remember and what we have forgotten, it has always seemed to me to be an act of arrogance and disrespect for people to say, "I know exactly how you feel," because they can't and they don't.

This sense of personal isolation and aloneness is exacerbated in victims of violence, especially when the victims are females from cultures that discount the voices, the values, and the experiences of women. Since the end of the war in Vietnam, there has been an upsurge in studies of many kinds of complex post-traumatic stress disorders, and most of them have found that what is most healing for victims of violence is the sense of commonality that arises from the sharing of experiences.[28]

I have no idea how Elena Segura Jiménez felt when she was being gang-raped and gang-sodomized, so I can only imperfectly imagine her fear and pain and shame. Many years ago, a wise older woman said to me (with more than a touch of irony in her voice), "You know, Susan, we do rather live in the body." I know this is true, and I also know that my own body and soul will always have scars from frequent and repeated acts of family violence carried out against me when I was a child.

I have described the acts and have even shown the two most readily visible scars to a therapist who, with the candor and self-disclosure that keep me trusting her, admits that she herself has never been the victim or intended victim of any physical violence. I wonder if she knows how fortunate and unusual she is and how she can never really go where clients who have experienced it have gone.

But here is the point: I have someone to talk to about my own inner and outer injuries, and the resources to pay her to listen and help, and the American feminist movement to support the telling of my stories, and the knowledge that the violence done to me was morally wrong in every way, and the possibility and actuality of healing. I used to have some odd pride that, unlike Elena, I never dissociated or "lost my mind" or went "another place inside" during the attacks on my body and that I remembered all the events. But as flashbacks and shadow memories continue to arise, I realize not only how little I actually know about the extent of what happened but also how familiar I am with the feeling of embedded pain.

Neither Elena Segura Jiménez nor any of the women whose asylum cases I heard used any words or conveyed any subtext that even remotely suggested self-pity. They spoke with a calmness and a plain descriptive ability that made my body ache then and still does.[29] When I look back on the almost eighteen years during which I heard them testify, I know that this was the time when I came to see firsthand the beauty and the lushness and the sweetness of the life of every woman in this world and to understand fully how we as women are all in it together, whether we want to be or not.

By having the resilience to survive the attacks, the presence of mind to notice their surroundings, and the courage to leave the places where they were harmed—and through the unadorned eloquence with which they asked for protection—the women like Elena who testified before me have given me the strength to examine my own life with greater integrity and compassion.

I have never suffered as they have, but in ways I only partially understand, they have *bentch*-pressed me and have surrounded me with the deep commonality that has the power to bless women survivors everywhere. In gratitude for what they gave to me, I bless each one of them in my mind, in my heart, and in my own strong and fragile body, and I do this with tears every day.

5. Persecution on Account of Political Opinion: Daniel Quetzal Monzon of Guatemala

Background

Perhaps no civil war in Central America has been as long as the one that laid waste to Guatemala from 1960 to 1996. During its thirty-six years, a number of governments came and went via coups and assassinations and fraudulent elections. More than 200,000 people, most of whom were members of indigenous groups, were murdered, and approximately 50,000 citizens simply became *los desaparecidos*, the disappeared ones, the vanished ones.

In October 1944, a coalition of university students, professors, school teachers, workers, liberals, and discontented members of the armed forces mounted a successful revolution against a military dictator who had refused to grant autonomy to and free expression in Guatemala's primary institution of higher learning, the University of San Carlos. For the next ten years, Guatemalans enjoyed expansions of educational opportunities at all levels, increased political freedoms, and an interest by the government in land redistribution and the concerns of peasants and workers.

In 1954, however, with the backing of the United States Central Intelligence Agency, which was concerned about what it perceived as leftist leanings in Guatemala, and with the encouragement of US agricultural companies fearful of having their profitable fruit businesses in Guatemala undermined, Colonel Carlos Castillo Armas led a successful coup against the democratically elected president, Jacobo Arbenz. Immediately, land reforms benefiting poor farmers were halted and reversed, and voting rights for those who could not read or write were revoked. Armas was assassinated in 1958, and his successor was no better.

In 1960, leftist guerrillas began battling the army. For the next six years, violence abounded, and many people were kidnapped, mutilated, and murdered. In 1966, a civilian government was elected, but the army eventually brought it down and saw to it that a promilitary president, Carlos Manuel Arana Osorio, was elected in 1970. For the next fifteen years, Guatemala was ruled and run by a succession of military governments that carried out atrocities against guerrilla groups, students, intellectuals, laborers, and innocent civilians. Soldiers loyal to these governments systematically slaughtered members of the many indigenous groups within the country, often dumping their mutilated bodies in public areas.

In 1985, a new constitution was drafted, but it was not until 1994 that peace talks between the government and the Guatemala Revolutionary National Unity began. In 1996, Álvaro Arzú was elected president in a run-off election, and peace accords that formally ended the long war were signed in December of that year.

In Court

Daniel Quetzal Monzon's name would have identified him as a descendant of the Maya even if his appearance had not. As his matronymic name suggested, he was from what is now called Quetzaltenango, a city founded by Maya thousands of years before

Spanish conquerors arrived in the sixteenth century. It is located in the southwestern quadrant of Guatemala in a mountain valley more than a mile above sea level, and the population is still largely indigenous. Many residents of the city refer to it as Xela (pronounced SHAY-la), a shortened version of its Mayan name.

Mr. Quetzal appeared for his asylum hearing in 1990 and was representing himself. Like most Guatemalans I saw in court, he was somewhat short in stature and appeared to be about five and a half feet tall. (Years later, I would hear one of his countrymen make a joke in court about organizing a Guatemalan basketball team at an immigration detention facility on the outskirts of Houston.) Mr. Quetzal had heavy eyelids and large earlobes, which two friends who worked for years as Peace Corps volunteers in Guatemala have told me are genetic characteristics of Maya. No doubt from countless hours in the sun, he was very tan, and he was wearing a T-shirt that said Happy Chanukah in both English and Hebrew, which I surmised he had obtained from a local thrift shop.

His asylum application listed his age as forty, and he had checked the box marked "political opinion" as the basis for his claim. In the space allotted for specifics, he had stated, "I was mistreated by the soldiers because I India," meaning, "because I am Indian." There was no supporting documentation attached to the application, and there were no witnesses to testify for him. The investigative summary submitted by the government's attorney before the hearing noted that Mr. Quetzal had been arrested during an INS raid of a roofing company.

When he had made his first appearance in court about a year earlier at a master calendar hearing, Mr. Quetzal had informed me that he spoke Spanish well and did not need an interpreter in either Quiché or Q'anjob'al, which were the only two Mayan dialects I had had any experience with in court. On the day of his asylum hearing, I verified with him that he did not need an interpreter in either of those dialects or in any of the more than fifty other Mayan languages spoken throughout Central America. But to be on the safe side, I went off the record and asked the court interpreter to speak with Mr. Quetzal for a few minutes in Spanish about *fútbol* (soccer) or some other neutral topic just to be entirely certain that we could go forward in Spanish.

On many prior occasions, respondents had assured me that they were proficient in English or some other language, only to become so nervous when testifying that they were forced to admit they needed an interpreter in their native language. In those situations, I had no choice but to postpone the case for many months and then start it all over with the appropriate interpreter when it finally came up on the docket again.

The interpreter told me that Mr. Quetzal was "good to go" in Spanish, so I gave the oath to start what I thought would be a relatively short hearing. The respondent began as follows:

> I am Daniel Quetzal Monzon, an Indian from Guatemala. I have learned to read and write, and I am not stupid. I walked here from my country eight years ago, and I want to stay, because if you send me back, they will kill me like they tried to do before. [Unclear pronoun references were common in testimony, just as they are in our speech, so I asked for a clarification of *they,* and I also asked Mr. Quetzal to try to back up his memory to the first time he had a problem in Guatemala and start from there.]
>
> *Sí*, it was in 1981, near Xela. My family all died young from sicknesses, so I lived by myself for many years in a small place near the edge of the city. I learned from an uncle how to work with wood, and I found jobs so I could buy food to eat and tires for my bicycle. I learned good Spanish from my customers [implying that he did carpentry for those of European descent within his city].

I kept up with politics, but I stayed away from it. It does no good. I could see that many people did not like us or each other, and death was all around. I was too old for the army and also for the guerrillas, so I thought I would be left alone.

In 1981—June or July, I think—I was coming home from work and turned down a little street to visit a friend and have a drink with him. There were soldiers in the street, and I saw them take two bodies from the back of a Jeep and throw them on the ground. I turned to go, but they saw me and chased me in their car till they got me. Two of them pulled me off my bike, and they ran over it with their car. Then they threw me in the Jeep where the bodies had been.

The rug in the car was soaked in blood, and there were fingers and a foot and a tongue still on the floor. I did not know what to do, but I tried at first to talk to the one who was driving. Before I could say many words, the soldiers put a rag in my mouth and a sack on my head and tied it tight around my neck. As we started driving, they would take turns hitting me in the head and calling me a dirty Indian and asking me why I dared to speak to them in Spanish.

I don't know how long we drove—maybe an hour—and all I could think about was how I had been captured by a death squad. I had heard of them, and now I was with them.

We finally got to some place in the mountains where I could smell the coolness, and for a moment I was not so afraid. The soldiers took me from the Jeep and made me walk ahead of them. I was still wearing the rag and the sack, so I fell down many times. They kicked me when I fell. I heard what sounded like a wooden gate, and then the rag and sack were taken and I was thrown into a cage. It was very dark by then, but I could hear the moans of other men.

When daylight came, I saw that I was in a wooden pen with five others of my people. I started to speak to them in our language, but they pointed to their injuries and wounds and motioned me to stop. One of them whispered to me in bad Spanish that we were all going to die. I was in the pen for two days without food or water, and no place to relieve myself.

Then they came for me. They tied my hands and feet to a wooden pole and carried me like a dead animal to a tent about a kilometer [six tenths of a mile] away. Inside they had a metal pole across the top. They took off all my clothes and burned them on the spot, and then they tied my hands above my head to the metal pole. My feet were still tied and not touching the ground, and I was hanging naked from this pole.

At first they beat me on my body with their clubs. I could hear my ribs break. Then one of them raised my feet and propped my ankles on the back of a chair. They beat me on the bottom of my feet. This had never happened to me before. Then they said, "It is time to find out about this Indian."

For the rest of the day, they interrogated me about my family, my job, and my friends, and no matter what I answered, they hit me again. I was almost unconscious, but then something changed my mind. [At this point, I was expecting Mr. Quetzal to testify that he had had a mental breakdown, but I was in error.]

I decided that if I was going to die, I would like for it to be with honor to my people. I have had a good life, and even though I do not care about politics, *me importan las cosas que vinieron a mi cuando nací.* I care about the things that came to me when I was born.

So when they asked me again which side I was loyal to, I told them that I was against the army and for the poor people and the students and the farmers and the Indians, and that everyone who wanted to should vote and no one should be killed. They laughed until they peed themselves, and then they told me they had something special for me.

They left for almost a day, and I stayed tied to the pole in the tent. When they came back, they had a battery. They put wires on my penis and in my anus, and they shocked me many times. Finally, they lowered my body enough to put my feet on the ground, and they hung a bucket of human shit around my testicles. The pain was great, and I passed out.

I woke up at night back in the pen, and there was nothing to be done. Two of the others had died since I was gone, and their bodies smelled bad in the heat. By daylight, I could see that some animals had gotten to them also.

I made up my mind to die, and I thought of my friends and my people. When I went to sleep, I did not expect to wake up again, but I heard noises and gunfire late in the afternoon and saw the soldiers running through the trees.

After some time, other men came and set me free. I guess they were guerrillas who chased the death squad away. Some of them gave me clothes, and they tied me to the back of a motorcycle and took me to a road where someone would find me. I don't remember much, but a man in a truck picked me up and took me to a church in my town. The priest took care of me for two weeks and would not let me out of the small room he made for me in the basement. He was also scared.

When I got home, I knew I could not stay because I did not want to be silent anymore. I started walking, and it took me two months to get here. Mexicans do not like Indians either, and I got beaten up twice in that country.

I have been working illegally. When I hear of other Indians from my country who are here, I go to meet them and try to help them out with clothes and food. It is not right what happened to us.

The INS attorney in court that day was an able lawyer and a decent man. Although I rarely looked at lawyers when someone was on the witness stand, I had glanced over during the most difficult part of Mr. Quetzal's testimony and had thought that the attorney looked ill. To my surprise and gratification, after Mr. Quetzal finished his direct testimony, the government's attorney immediately volunteered that he would waive cross-examination and would not oppose a grant of asylum on the ground of political opinion "or on any other ground on which Your Honor sees fit to base it." It was with great relief that I told Mr. Quetzal that his request for asylum was granted on the basis of the political opinion he had formulated and expressed to the death squad. He received the information with dignified tears and gratitude, promising me he would "get my paperwork done and become legal."

I was always deeply satisfied when a government attorney fulfilled his or her ethical obligation to see that justice is done, and I would always note that on the record. After court was adjourned, I went back to my office but could do no work. I later found out that the government's attorney had gone back to his office and vomited on his desk.

Reflection

In a dark time, the eye begins to see …
—Theodore Roethke

They say that a healthy adult human heart weighs about twelve ounces, but after I finished hearing Mr. Quetzal's testimony, mine felt as if it weighed twelve pounds. What happened to him was one of the worst cases of sustained torture and man's inhumanity to man that I heard in my eighteen years on the bench. And as I thought about its emotional effect on me as well as its blessing, two things emerged, and both have surprised me enormously.

My first reflection about this case concerns how wounded men are, and how my even saying that is an implicit acknowledgment of what a shallow understanding I had of that damage for so many years.

Few people of intelligence and conscience would deny that the feminist and lesbian feminist and gay rights movements—and the legitimate scholarship that has arisen from each of them—have done much to illuminate the history of gender inequality and to open up American society to some sober thinking about how badly the 51 percent who are women and the 10 percent who are homosexual have been treated by the heterosexual male population.

In the early days of American feminism in the 1960s, instances of verbal male-bashing were common, and although many of the statements were true in their content, they were sometimes said or shouted with a kind of mean-spiritedness or even venom that served only to undermine their potential effectiveness. Then lesbian feminists seized the metaphorical microphone, and to the many justified criticisms of men we added condemnation of heterosexual women who continued to "sleep with the enemy." And as if rhetoric were not already at the shrillest pitch and highest decibel, lesbian separatism took shape, and many women decided they would have nothing whatsoever to do with men, at least until a plumber was needed to fix the toilet at the all-dyke rural commune.

Like Zionism, lesbian separatism made a certain amount of sense to me for a while, and although I never decamped to a collective living arrangement with other women, I certainly viewed men with suspicion, could not understand why they would not immediately grasp and implement total equality for women, and generally held them in low regard, notwithstanding overwhelming evidence that many of their accomplishments benefited everyone and had not been attained on the backs of women.

My shoddy elitism changed dramatically one day in 1979 when I was teaching a class about feminist legal issues at the University of Massachusetts in Amherst. Most of the women in the class were very bright and radical young feminists from the university as well as from Smith College and Hampshire College, which were part of a five-college consortium in the area. But the class also had two male students, neither of whom was there for the interloping or voyeuristic purposes ascribed to them by some of the women, and one of whom, David, was academically and intellectually far ahead of everyone else. The reading assignment for this particular class had been parts of Susan Brownmiller's groundbreaking book *Against Our Will: Men, Women, and Rape.*[30]

My format as a teacher was to lecture for twenty-five minutes, spend the next five minutes taking a position and inviting a response, and then use the remaining twenty minutes encouraging and moderating a discussion among the students about the subject of the lecture. I remember talking about Brownmiller's theory that rape is not a sex crime but is instead a raw crime of violence, a gender-based hate crime, and a political crime of power over women.

As I opened up the discussion, the first remark from one of the more radical women was, "All men are rapists." I recognized this as a line uttered by a fictional character in Marilyn French's novel *The Women's Room,*[31] but I had never heard it said out loud or put forward as a theory by any serious feminist, and I was taken aback.

Even though I was angry at the many examples of sexism in the culture at large (not to mention the ones that crowd the halls of higher education), I generally thought of myself as being fair-minded, and I considered the student's assertion to be not only extreme and defamatory but also categorically untrue. In the interest of academic freedom, however, I decided to allow her to elaborate on her statement. But before I could do so, David said, "Now wait a minute. I can't let that one pass. I want to respond to it."

What followed was a short but eloquent defense of decent men who do not and would not rape women, a description of the love and respect he felt for his mother and many other women, his remorse about how badly women had been treated throughout history, his growing awareness of some of his own sexist thinking and behaviors, and his sense of being thoroughly offended at having been lumped in with violent men who harm women.

As I watched this young man say what he did with control and courage and self-respect, something in me shifted enormously, and I knew I was seeing and hearing a better future for women and men together than I had ever thought possible. And even more importantly, I also knew that my own descent into irrational radicalism had stopped, that there were and would be men worth listening to, and that I would never be a balanced human being if I continued to mindlessly devalue the other 49 percent of the population.

Despite the fourteen-year difference in our ages, David and I became good friends over the next ten years, and in 1997 I was overjoyed to attend his wedding in California to a feminist who is as intelligent and insightful as he is.

Whether it was sitting on a West Village park bench sharing a pie from John's Pizzeria on Bleecker Street while David was in law school, or watching him play his guitar and juggle on a corner near New York University, or seeing him learn and practice sign language so he could communicate with his hearing-impaired nephew, or listening to him talk about his hopes and plans and troubles and disappointments, I was changed for the better every time I was with this man, and I was somehow able to catch a glimpse of the pressures and prisons that men's expected societal and familial and business and military roles have surrounded them with.

Through David, I began to develop some real and much-needed compassion for men, and although I still laugh when I think of funny feminist one-liners, such as "A woman without a man is like a fish without a bicycle" or "Men were invented because cats don't do yard work," I nevertheless know that seeing beyond our genitals to the deeper wounds of both women and men is one of the linchpins of a more peaceful world.

Having had much of my thinking and most of my generalizations about men corrected by David, I began to notice how violent men can be toward other men, and as I recently began working my way through my reflections about Daniel Quetzal Monzon, I spent dozens of hours with the anthology *Crimes of War 2.0: What the Public Should Know.*[32] It includes accounts of many of the things endured by Mr. Quetzal, but it also explicates other horrors that do not readily come to our American minds when we think of war: biological and medical experiments, chemical weapons and gases, cluster and carpet bombs, and ethnic cleansing.

It is impossible to read or even browse through the book without realizing that the world's many swamplands of cruelty and theme parks of torture are filled with far more than just bullets and grenades, that almost all of it is the invention of men and not of women, and that the intended targets are chiefly other men. The creators of these methods and instruments of destruction (many of whom are American scientists) argue that their weapons and tactics of overkill are necessary to keep up with other nations' developments in military technology or to protect our families and our way of life.

Such arguments, however, are little more than transparent bureau-speak and jingoism for perpetuating Americanism and traditional sex roles, and they are fundamentally driven by the collective insanity of a thriving military-industrialism that urges men to spend billions of dollars and hours and careers devising ever more lethal ways to kill other men. In a society and a world order that are already rigged against the physical and emotional health of both women and men, I don't find these rationalizations to be anything other than a cause for heart-sickening sorrow.

The second thread of reflection that unspooled from Mr. Quetzal's case originated from his saying to himself, "I care about the things that came to me when I was born," and then squarely telling his captors that he was against them and what they represented.

In my view, the majority of Mr. Quetzal's testimony more strongly supported a grant of asylum based on his membership in a particular social group (indigenous Indians) than on the political opinion he had checked off on his asylum application. But I was so moved by the workings of his courage—and by the personal alchemy that had transformed his individual situation into a strong and unequivocal statement against the army and in support of everyone in his country who was downtrodden and disenfranchised—that I chose instead to predicate the grant on his political opinion, which the application itself had designated as the basis of his claim.

Beyond the confines of the case, however, the internal realization that prompted Mr. Quetzal's verbal metamorphosis has stayed with me, and I have often tried to identify and list the things that came to me when I was born and then decide whether I still care about them.

The best thing that came to me when I was born was a loving grandmother, who was the only woman in my life ever to tell me that I was beautiful. By conventional standards, I am not and never have been, but it was wonderful to often be told so by her, even though I know she was very biased because I was her first grandchild.

She lived a hundred and twenty miles from us, and I was only with her every few months and on holidays. But her kindness and constancy and physical affection saw me through a terrible and violent childhood, and other than not knowing how to actually do it, the only thing that kept me from becoming a child suicide was the

Susan L. Yarbrough

knowledge that it surely would have killed her too. I loved her and cared about her with all my heart and still do, and I want every child to be born with such a safe and steady person in his or her life.

I don't think of myself as a mystic, but I believe I sometimes have visitations from her in the nighttime dreamscapes that my unconscious constructs and unfolds for me. She is usually about sixty years old, and she speaks to me briefly in short, declarative sentences, such as, "That's the one," or, "You know better," or, "I'll wait." The power of her presence is so palpable that I always wake up crying and smelling the scent of the soap and perfume she used.

My grandmother was fifty-one when I was born, and my earliest recollection of her is of her long gray hair that she wore up in a horizontal roll that traced the hairline of her neck. I still don't understand how hairpins held it up, but I loved watching her let it down and brush it out every night. To this day, I have never colored my own hair and have enjoyed watching it turn gray like hers. And although a few friends encourage me to add more zip to my limited wardrobe, I can usually be found wearing a gray T-shirt or sweatshirt simply because I find the color so soothing.

My grandmother's death on May 15, 1980, occasioned the only episode of dissociation I've ever experienced. I was living in Massachusetts at the time, and when my father finally called to tell me about her, it was too late to get to Boston or Hartford and catch a flight to Texas in time for her funeral the following day.

The next two weeks are a blank to me. Fortunately, I had finished grading all the term papers and final exams for the courses I had taught during the spring semester, and I vaguely remember giving the grade sheets to another faculty member who lived nearby so she could take them to the appropriate office at the university. But other than that, I recall nothing until I found myself on June 1 running a familiar ten-mile route through the Berkshires, feeling completely unmoored from life, and having a disquieting sense that I would

94

thereafter be working without a net. My grandmother was a gift that came to me when I was born, and I care for it and treasure it each day.

Another thing that came to me when I was born was a God consciousness, and I also care about it and keep it alive within me.

A relatively new field of academic study is neurotheology, and it has generated several controversial theories and a growing body of provocative research about whether belief in something transcendent is hardwired into our DNA. Geneticists, neuroscientists, and cell biologists have all contributed their own "proof,"[33] but I think it was in poetry that I first saw written evidence of the God gene I had felt since I began to have words and to form ideas and thoughts about what is transcendent.

In his well-known ode "Intimations of Immortality from Recollections of Early Childhood,"[34] the poet William Wordsworth describes us at our births as "trailing clouds of glory" as we "come / From God, who is our home." The very next line exuberantly declares, "Heaven lies about us in our infancy!" But the somber line after that says, "Shades of the prison-house begin to close," until finally the vision and the God-trailings we are born with "fade into the light of common day."

I had no moments of wonder as a child, because safety was never a given, and wonder requires a certain amount of psychic space and amplitude in which to bloom. Most of my days and nights were filled with real and imagined fears, and I was always fighting a rearguard action against assaults of several kinds.

I could not figure out why so many harmful things were happening to me, but the inside-out blessing of this was that I held on to some childish belief that there was a God who was seeing all of it, thinking it was wrong, and planning how to save me from it someday. And even when that didn't occur, I still believed and have never quit believing, even though I eventually got frighteningly angry at God for stranding me in a family that silently colluded in a parent's relentless use of me as a target for scapegoating, shunning, draconian punishments, and capricious brutality.

Maybe I kept on with God as a default setting: my grandmother was not nearby, I was isolated within my family, I was actively prevented from choosing friends, and I had no trustworthy adult to confide in. Who the hell else was I going to talk to and believe in?

When I look back on all this, I am surprised at how strongly I did and still do believe, and how as an adult I have been able to open myself to experiences of wonder, reverence, and the joys of connecting with the soul of nature and the heartbeats of other human beings. I don't see the light of any day as common, and I often sense that I am recovering the vision and momentary heaven that came to me when I was born. I care about them more than I can say in words.

There were, of course, other things I was born with—the English language, for example, with its Latinate vocabulary and its Germanic tongue, both of which give it such muscle and elegance and expressiveness—and I am certainly grateful for that. But I have less certitude and clarity about the importance and intrinsic value of several other birth-things than I do about my grandmother and my God consciousness and my ongoing intoxication with words.

Being born with an adequate brain and a healthy body into a white, middle-class family meant that I was able to get a good education, although when I was accepted into graduate school, my parents hastened to tell me that they would not assist me financially (I had not even asked them to) because "you are already the most overeducated female we know." Later, when I began putting myself through law school, they reminded me of their beliefs that "women have no place outside the home" and that I would most likely be reduced to "having to find some ol' boy to marry so he can support you." They were also fond of telling my sister and me about what a privilege it was to be born in a free country like America, but I have often felt far more free in tolerant countries like Canada and the Netherlands than I have in my own.

I don't discount the external circumstances of my birth as blessings, but they don't seem as significant in the trajectory of my life as having had a tender grandmother with whom to form a human attachment or a God consciousness that continues to serve as an organizing principle of accountability, companionship, and awe.

With these thoughts in mind, I see that the blessings of Daniel Quetzal Monzon in my life are a clearer view of the harm done to innocent men by other men, as well as a greater gratitude and sense of care for the important things that came to me when I was born.

Just as I will never again underestimate the variety and the tools of evil or the extent to which decent men have been harmed by all the forces that war against their growth into wholeness, I will also never underestimate the ability of one loving person to save the life of a child, or the power of a single trailing glimmer of something greater than myself to mediate hope and to light up every common day.

Afterword

I've never felt a pain that didn't bear a blessing.
—Gene Knudsen Hoffman

And even in our sleep, pain which cannot forget
falls drop by drop upon the heart,
until, in our own despair, against our will,
comes wisdom through the awful grace of God.
—Aeschylus

Do not be daunted by the enormity of the world's grief.
Do justly, now. Love mercy, now. Walk humbly, now.
You are not obligated to complete the work,
but neither are you free to abandon it.
—The Talmud (attributed)

I retired from my job as a judge on July 31, 2005, and like many new retirees, I spent the first month sleeping till 8:00 a.m., lingering over coffee and the newspaper, showering late, going without makeup and jewelry, puttering around the house, playing Scrabble on the computer, exploring a few cultural venues and events, making some dinners for my partner who was still working, staying up late watching a little junk TV, and generally feeling let out of jail. I notified the State Bar of Texas that I wanted to go on inactive status as an attorney, and I bought a cremation policy so I wouldn't have to worry about anything as messy as death. In short, I was ready to relax and have some fun for the next thirty years.

But on Labor Day, I woke up screaming from a nightmare in which I was sitting on top of a volcano that was about to erupt, and as far as my eyes could see there stretched a line consisting of every person I had seen in court for the past eighteen years. Because caseloads had always been heavy, it was not unusual for me to meet and interact with two thousand new people every year, so the line in the dream was quite long. All of them were waiting to tell me something important and to ask for my help, and in the dream it was imperative that I speak with each one of them before the volcano blew and we were all swept away in a tide of molten lava that emptied into a filthy river.

As I began to talk fast in the hope that I could meet everyone's needs and save all the people, the volcano erupted and the lava flowed rapidly downhill, carrying us into the polluted river. Then, as the river rushed and cascaded farther downward through muddy rapids, it was eventually blocked from emptying into a placid sea by a series of locks and dams, and the toxicity of the waters in which I and the others were floating quickly killed us all.

I had had other nightmares in my life, most of them having to do with my parents, but only two of those had recurred often, so I thought that the volcano dream was destined to be a one-trick pony that would yield itself easily to the psychological techniques of association and amplification. In other words, I would take it apart, find out its meaning, think no more about it, and be forever free of the intense anxiety and nausea and terror and sweat and sense of suffocation with which I had awoken from it.

But that did not happen, and as I filled retirement days productively with reading, Silver Sneakers exercise classes at the YMCA, community service, and helping my partner's recently moved parents become acquainted with Houston, by night I had more unsettling dreams as well as many repetitions of the volcano nightmare.

During most of my thirty years in the legal profession, I had gotten up at five every morning in order to have time to read, pray, walk, and get ready for work, and I was usually so tired by early evening that I was almost always gratefully in bed by 9:00 p.m. It was important to me to be able to work with intensity and focus and concentration, so I refused to go out on "school nights," and many of my friends thought I was a hopeless fuddy-duddy.

Put simply, I had always welcomed bed and sleep, but not anymore, and I began to consciously look for ways to avoid the unconsciousness of sleep, such as late-night runs to a drive-through Starbucks for a decaf grande nonfat latte, followed by re-reruns of *M.A.S.H.* and *Mission: Impossible* on a retro TV channel, followed by more reading and puttering and finally a drift into uneasy sleep, followed by a waking headache every morning and circadian rhythms gone completely awry.

I knew something subterranean was going on, but I chose to ignore it. So when the opportunity arose for me to become involved on a daily basis in the care and transportation of an elderly acquaintance who had developed leukemia, I volunteered to become her constant companion through long hours at a cancer hospital, and I let myself become absorbed in the mysteries of her platelet counts rather than in the churnings of my own psyche. Her death at the end of seven months caused me to experience a loss of role and usefulness, and I began to see that I had no choice but to face the demons rising up from continuing nightmares and bad dreams about work.

I found a therapist and tried to start talking, only to realize that she could not even say the word *lesbian* and was more interested in why I was overweight than she was in my bad dreams, my anxiety and depression and panic attacks, and what I had done in my former job. Other than in my first session with her, she took no notes, was usually late, left her cell phone on and answered it when any of her adult children called, and often complained about how poorly she was reimbursed by insurance companies. I wearily gave up on her after eight months and then turned my attention to the fact that my partner of sixteen years had decided to leave our relationship on a month's notice.

When May 1, 2009, arrived, I was alone, filled with despair, and still very frightened by my dreams and what they might be telling me. I knew that I had been a good judge and a fair judge, and I simply did not understand why I could not just enjoy the satisfaction of having worked hard and done well and then get on with the rest of my life.

In October, my former partner asked if I would like to go with her to a weekend marriage workshop to see if there was any way we could work things out and possibly get back together. I agreed to do so, and at the end of the event we decided to try couples counseling with one of the therapists who had conducted the workshop. We saw him together a few times, and then each of us saw him separately.

At the conclusion of my solo session with him, he told me that he had done three tours of duty as a helicopter pilot in Vietnam and that he believed I had primary post-traumatic stress disorder from childhood violence and injuries at home, as well as secondary post-traumatic stress disorder from the many things I had heard and absorbed during my work as a judge. He recommended that I start seeing another therapist who was skilled in trauma issues, and I began doing that on November 3, 2009.

Before I ever set foot in her office, however, I thought about what I could have done to avoid being where I was right then mentally, and I recalled that every year at the annual judges' conference the front office had brought in a psychologist to talk about judicial stress. He had made the same vapid presentation year after year and had always approvingly included the example of one judge who, when he got annoyed or frustrated with people in court, would imagine taking out an Uzi assault rifle from under the bench and spraying everyone in the courtroom with gunfire.

I had never put this abhorrent suggestion into practice, but I realized as I drove toward my first appointment with the new therapist that I did indeed have a stress disorder and that I needed a lot more help than I had ever thought I did. For the past three years, I have been talking once or twice a week to her as if my life depended on it, and in some ways it does.

The first asylum case I heard after I was sworn in was that of a South Vietnamese young man whose grandfather had saved his life by pushing him under a bag of rice when the village was invaded and pillaged and burned by the Viet Cong in early 1975. The young man had been five at the time, and the grandfather had survived the attack by feigning death. After the rebels departed, there was no one else left alive in the village, and most of the dead had been dismembered and decapitated with machetes.

Some American troops in retreat toward Saigon rumbled through later in the day, picked up the boy and his grandfather, and made Polaroid pictures of family members whose bodies had been hacked up and whose severed heads had been impaled on bamboo poles in front of the family hut. As they dropped off the two survivors at a refugee assembly point, the soldiers gave the photos to the boy as souvenirs, and twelve years later they were offered into evidence at the asylum hearing before me.

I had seen hundreds if not thousands of photographic images of the war in Vietnam, but now fifteen of them were right here in front of me in faded color and were crucial pieces of evidence in determining whether this young man could stay in my country or would have to return to what was left of his. I took it all in, and I never stopped letting in the details and specifics and gory pictures and gruesome oral and written descriptions in every other asylum case for another eighteen years. There were many days when I left work feeling like I had no skin.

My swearing-in took place in November of 1987. Three months earlier, there had been a week's training session for new US immigration judges, but the next one was not scheduled until the spring of 1989. By the time I attended it, I had been on the bench for eighteen months and had not had one day of official training. The learning curve had been steep and the hours long, but I felt like I had made my way to a good practical and intellectual understanding of the job.

I don't know what I expected from the training, but I remember that there was some role-playing, dozens of handouts, a few dry lectures, and absolutely nothing about how to personally and emotionally handle the evidence of torture and persecution that I was seeing every day. As I had done with every other piece of violence in my life, I buried all of it, and when I finally retired, the volcano erupted.

About a year ago, a friend told me she had read somewhere that the difference between sadness and depression is this: depression is when nothing matters, and sadness is when everything matters. This has been a useful distinction to me and has helped me realize that what lay beneath my own volcano was tremendous sadness about how damaging the world is to so many people, how much that has always mattered to me, and how powerless I had been to hear or save more than just a few of them.

Psychologists, especially those influenced by Carl Jung, place great value on recognizing, integrating, and even welcoming the constituents of one's own shadow. This shadow is often mistakenly thought of as only the darker parts of ourselves, but it is more accurately all the parts of ourselves that we have disowned or not yet brought to consciousness.

For example, one darker part of my shadow I have reluctantly had to own is the schadenfreude I experience when something unfortunate happens to someone I don't like, such as the time I felt a perverse delight when George W. Bush wrecked his mountain bike (which he was pedaling when he should have been governing) and sustained minor scratches and bruises to his face. More seriously and importantly, a better part of my shadow that I disowned because of my job was the ability to feel deep pleasure when I see even the smallest good at work in the world, and I am now giving careful attention to bringing that part into the light of awareness.

This book is both more and less than what I thought it would be, and I have easily concluded that less is more. I originally intended to write about three cases demonstrating each of the five grounds of asylum eligibility, and in contemplation of this I began frequenting one of the major research libraries in Texas in order to do further extensive reading about Bosnia, China, Iran, Ethiopia, and the Punjab region of India.

But as I thought about the fifteen people whose stories I planned to tell, the five who appear in this book stepped decisively toward me mentally and emotionally, and I realized that extended accounts of fifteen people who had suffered greatly would not only numb the reader but would also reignite my own sadness and nightmares. More than all the others, these are the five who brought me to my knees in grief, in anger, and in prayer.

Which somehow brings me around again to the many facets of the word *blessing* and my certainty that none of the five asylees in this book intended to give me one, but each of them did it nonetheless and unawares, even though I was initially oblivious to the gifts and blessings they were bestowing on me. It was not until I was broken open by the tenderness and innocence of Josué Maldonado Ortiz that my own blindness and deafness could begin to escape through the cracks. And it was only then that I began to feel a common humanity with everyone who asked me for asylum, to incorporate the lessons of their lives into mine, and to receive their blessings with a wideness of heart I would not have thought possible.

I have never minded getting older, mostly because it makes all the harm and loneliness of childhood seem farther away. Lately, however, aging has taken on a very affirmative feeling for me, largely because I see that the older I get, the more I notice how blessings have entered and continue to enter my life in so many different guises and disguises.

What once looked like an ugly facial scar turns out to be a reminder of childhood resilience. What once felt like the unlivable losses of greatly wanted children through two miscarriages in my mid-thirties has opened up spaces in my life for me to hold and cherish the dozens of children and grandchildren of friends. What once appeared to be a devastating departure by a beloved partner has led me in a roundabout journey over a broken road to many open doors and to a life-giving therapist who continues to help me find those doors, frame them, and then walk through them with that paradoxical mix of fear and love that lets me know I am going and growing in the right direction. And what once seemed to be the unbearable weight of thousands of hours spent in listening to asylum cases and their attendant proofs of torture and persecution has, at last, transformed itself into a soulful and far-reaching lesson in how to welcome strangers, including those parts of myself from which I was and continue to be estranged.

At the time I heard the cases described in this book, the only emotions I could readily identify within myself were pain and anger about what had happened to those who had been harmed, along with some sense of personal release and temporary lightening at being able to give them relief and hope.

Immediately after I granted any asylum application and extended welcome and good wishes to the person who had been persecuted,

I would rush out of the courtroom and into my office, lock the door, and cry for about half an hour. The two words that would always form underneath my tears were *thank you*—to the Creator for bringing me to that day, for ears to hear, and for a painful and heartbreaking job that nevertheless gave me the power to spare someone's life. But it wasn't until I retired from the day-to-day physical hearing of the cases that I began to really hear and feel the sounds and echoes and harmonics and overtones of the blessings they brought and are still bringing to my life.[35]

In the process of putting this book together, I have often needed to take breaks to calm myself. Typically, this has involved settling into my trusty recliner and listening with headphones to peaceful music, such as orchestral largos and adagios, or lush and slow-paced choral works, or even some benign New Age instrumental pieces that I use in my massage practice.

But as the writing took me further into multiple levels of awareness of the many ways in which my life has been amplified and deepened by those whose cases I heard, I began to listen almost exclusively to a recording of twenty-five Tibetan singing bowls,[36] for it would immediately transport me into aural layers of sound and tone and vibration that morphed into the resonating voices and spirits of those who had shared their fears and their longings with me as they took the witness stand next to my bench.

So here are Esteban Marcial Mosqueda, Josué Maldonado Ortiz, Khalid Talhami, Elena Segura Jiménez, and Daniel Quetzal Monzon—those who came out of great tribulation caused by color, faith, nationality, womanhood, and political chaos. Each one was with me at the fiery volcano, each is now with me on a peaceful sea, and all of them are lasting sources of light and courage and hope that cascade around me every day.

By letting me see their lives and their pain, they have let me become more in contact with my own; and by letting me see their joy and gratitude in finding safe haven, they have let me know my own happiness and thankfulness for the places of refuge and asylum in my own life. Because of them, I am truly *bentch*-pressed—held firmly and securely by goodness and blessings rather than awash in muddy rivers of darkness and evil, and this tectonic shift has caused me to make enormous and much-needed changes in things as mundane as my choices in reading and entertainment as well as in more important choices about relationships and the spending of what precious time might be left.

Besides the act of saying a heartfelt "I love you" to another sentient being, my greatest interpersonal pleasure in life has come from being able to look into someone's eyes while holding their face or their hands in my own hands and to say, "I am a better person because of you." If I could physically do that now with these five who touched me so deeply, I would. But because I do not know or even need to know where they are and how they are, it must be and is sufficient for me to hold them in my mind's eye and my heart's beat and my soul's breath, and to *bentch* them in this way:

May you be peaceful.
May you be happy.
May you always be safe from harm.
May you set your tents among us.
May you know that you are remembered.
And may you be blessed as you have blessed me.
Amen.

Acknowledgments

When I think of all the people who have helped, encouraged, taught, and inspired me during my sixty-five years, I am overwhelmed with gratitude, and I want to acknowledge as many of them as I can remember. Because all of them were or are such plainspoken and unpretentious people who eschew honorifics, and also because they are all still so present with me in my mind and heart, I am stating their names without specifying either their professional titles or whether they are still physically alive.

I begin by thanking my academic teachers: Mrs. Livarre (the best first-grade teacher any child or parent could hope for), Claire King, Dan Jenkins, Rufus Spain, Ann Miller, Euell Porter, Irene Rosenberg, and Sidney Buchanan. I also thank my in-person spiritual teachers, whose very presence shed light: Dan McGee, Riley Eubank, Bill Kerley, Elie Wiesel, Stephen Levine, Suzan Cotellesse, Hope Lipnick, and James Hollis. And I am equally thankful for those spiritual teachers whom I have never met but whose lessons have sustained me over the years: Mohandas Gandhi, Wayne Muller, Rachel Cowan, Rachel Naomi Remen, Viktor Frankl, Rainer Maria Rilke, David Whyte, Abraham Joshua Heschel, Joseph Soleveitchik, and Rami Shapiro.

My twelve years as a trial and appellate lawyer gave me deep gratitude for those attorneys who taught me how to practice law with intelligence and decency: Bob Broom, Mary Clarkson, Janet Fink, Nan Kripke, Michael Gage, Wendy Lauring, Diana Budzanoski,

Arthur Cambouris, William Hellerstein, Bill Bellotti, Ellen Fried, Gerald Ryan, and Daniel Hedges. During my eighteen years as a judge, I was continually inspired by the integrity and skills of those colleagues who brought more than just their brains into the courtroom, and my personal and professional debt to them is enormous: Stephanie Marks, Alan Page, Richard Brodsky, Annie Sue Garcy, Dana Marks, Alan Vomacka, Craig Zerbe, Bette Stockton, John Gossart, Patricia Sheppard, Michael Bennett, and Joe Vail. Every day I was on the bench, I was reminded of how much more difficult my work would have been without those interpreters and administrators and court staff who did their jobs with patience and sensitivity and who treated everyone with dignity, and I hope they heard and sensed my great appreciation for them: Lucrecia Hug, Adele LaPinelle, Modesto Canales, Haydee Nieto, Rod Prado, Richard Plowman, Noemi Sanchez, Tom Davis, Tammy Young, Elise Canfield, Josie Corder, Ben Romero, Christina Reyes, Mary Gallegos, Marta Tijerina, Ariel Nguyen, and Rafiqullah Rahman. I am especially indebted to Teresa Rose for reviewing and correcting the Spanish names, words, phrases, and sentences that appear in this book. I am also grateful for those government attorneys who saw that justice was done and for those private and public-sector attorneys who represented asylum-seekers with zeal and integrity.

I would lack emotional equilibrium were it not for those who have listened carefully when my heart was troubled: Ruth Jean Eisenbud, Barbara Ellman, and the one to whom this book is dedicated. And I would lack perspective and good sense were it not for my students who taught me so well: David Ebert, Jill Tregor, Debbie Wald, and Amira Rahman. I am thankful for all of them.

Of the people in my biological family, I am most grateful for my sister Julie and my maternal grandmother, Lona Cotton Futrell. They have been the glue and the thread that held the shards and remnants together. And I am grateful for Angela, who shared sixteen years and her family with me.

Thankfulness seems like an almost shallow concept when I think of those friends who have stayed the course with me even when I appeared to be off-course: Kathy Crawley, F.S. "Jumpy" Lentz, Dianne Neal, Fran Avera, Jim Avera, Virginia Failing, Mollie Oliphant, Marianne Tomecek, Jolanda Wood-Reeves, Barbara Loeser, Jerry Schwartz, Dori Poole Schwartz, Gregory, and Arthur Passaretti. I hope they know how much they mean to me.

In the nonhuman realm of sentient beings, I am grateful for my peaceful dog Farley (the name he came with) who looks like the business end of a dust mop and should have been named Velcro because of how he clings to me. As I was beginning to write this book, my beloved mutt Willie died at the age of fourteen, and I swore I would not get another dog until after all the writing was done. Two weeks later, I saw Farley on the website of a local organization that rescues shaggy dogs, and I resisted his charms for three days before bringing him home with me. We enrolled in training classes, and he soon became a therapy dog who delights people in hospitals and nursing homes. He is the soul of calmness and affection, and as is usually the case for people who love dogs, he often provides rescue and therapy for me.

Throughout all of my life, I have been and remain most thankful for that spirit and presence I call God but who goes by many names to many people. Although there are those who think that faith is an opiate or that belief in a higher being is a function of some unhealthy parental introject or psychological need, for me it is a choice, for I can't imagine that being alive today and feeling connected to every person on earth are anything but gifts and graces from a great and embracing universal heart.

Notes

1. David Spangler, *Blessing: The Art and the Practice* (New York: Riverhead Books, 2002), pp. 21, 19, 39, 44.

2. Lionel Corbett, *The Sacred Cauldron: Psychotherapy as a Spiritual Practice* (Wilmette, IL: Chiron Publications, 2011), pp. 20, 21.

3. Dan Wakefield, quoted in June Mack Maffin, *Soulistry— Artistry of the Soul* (Alresford, UK: Circle Books, 2011), p. 21.

4. Evangelos Christou, *The Logos of the Soul* (Zurich: Spring Publications, 1976).

5. Corbett, *Sacred Cauldron*, pp. 159–60.

6. Although this quotation is widely attributed to nineteenth-century Danish novelist Karen Blixen (nom de plume Isak Dinesen), it does not appear in Dinesen's work. Instead, it is the inspirational epigraph to the chapter entitled "Action" in *The Human Condition* by political theorist Hannah Arendt (Chicago: The University of Chicago Press, 1958), p. 175. Arendt's book mentions Dinesen in several places.

7. Terry Tempest Williams, "Why I Write," in *Writing Creative Nonfiction*, eds. Carolyn Forché and Philip Gerard (Cincinnati: Story Press, 2001), pp. 6–7.

8. See generally John Rawls, *A Theory of Justice* (Cambridge, MA: Belknap Press of Harvard University, 1971). This difficult and seminal work in the field of political philosophy raises many questions about fairness, impartiality, tolerance, the basis of

equality, distributive justice, and the concept of a well-ordered society. Most available scholarship that has sought to apply Rawlsian principles and concepts to immigration has done so in the context of migration itself and not in the context of what the legal system of a host or receiving country should or should not provide for illegal immigrants within its borders.

9. Forché and Girard, *Creative Nonfiction*, p. 1.

10. "Tell all the Truth but tell it slant—," in *The Complete Poems of Emily Dickinson*, ed. Thomas H. Johnson (Boston: Little, Brown, 1960), p. 1129.

11. For an excellent overview of race-based discrimination in Cuba, see Mark Q. Sawyer, *Racial Politics in Post-Revolutionary Cuba* (New York: Cambridge University Press, 2006). *Pigmentocracy,* a term I had not heard before reading Sawyer's book, is described as "racial hierarchy based on skin shade and the African-ness of facial features" (pp. 136–38).

12. Peggy McIntosh, Working Paper 189, "White Privilege and Male Privilege: A Personal Account of Coming to the Correspondences through Work in Women's Studies" (Wellesley College Center for Research on Women, 1988), later excerpted in the Winter 1990 issue of the journal *Independent School.*

13. "All the Hemispheres," in *A Year with Hafiz*, ed. and trans. Daniel Landinsky (New York: Penguin Books, 2010), p. 356.

14. "Address to the Nation on United States Policy in Central America May 9, 1984," *The Public Papers of President Ronald W. Reagan*, Ronald Reagan Presidential Library, accessed September 14, 2011, www.reagan.utexas.edu/archives/speeches/1984/50984h.htm.

15. I first heard (and still hear) this phrase from Reverend William C. Kerley, a friend and guide for more than forty years. He teaches a Sunday-morning class called "Ordinary Life" at St. Paul's United Methodist Church in Houston, Texas, and his weekly lessons can be found at www.ordinarylife.org. Bill sheds

good light for his students to follow, and he is one of a growing number of Protestant clergy who recognize that Jesus was first and foremost a radical Jew and that Christianity cannot be fully grasped without an understanding of Judaism.

16. "(Ours is a) Simple Faith" can be found on Mustard Retreat's compact disc *MR7* (Yellow Room Records, 2005). The song can also be heard on YouTube.

17. See George Lakoff and Mark Johnson, *Metaphors We Live By* (Chicago: University of Chicago Press, 1980). A much more entertaining and accessible treatment of the same topic is James Geary's recent *I Is an Other: The Secret Life of Metaphor and How It Shapes the Way We See the World* (New York: HarperCollins, 2011).

18. In her strong and graceful (and often humorous) book *An Altar in the World: A Geography of Faith* (New York: HarperOne, 2009), Episcopal priest Barbara Brown Taylor notes that the Hindu Upanishads describe God as "Thou Before Whom All Worlds Recoil." The vastness implicit in such a concept prompted her to think of God as "the More, the Really Real, the Luminous Web That Holds Everything in Place" (p. 7).

19. I have not been able to find the origin of the term *Great Seamstress,* but I have heard it used in more than one sermon in the past few years (possibly because it is readily available to clergy at www. onlinepulpit.ivpress.com/2010/07/god_the_seamstress.php).

20. This verse is from the Jewish Publication Society's translation of the Hebrew Bible (Philadelphia: 1985).

21. Luke 10:25–37 in the New Testament. As a matter of actual fact, the road leading away from Jerusalem to Jericho has always been a perilous one as it winds and descends almost four thousand feet in its eighteen miles through rocky and hilly terrain. It is a dangerous drive today, and in the first century it was a place where bandits often accosted and physically harmed travelers.

22. These are the last two lines of "Questions of a Worker Who Reads" (originally titled "Fragen eines lesenden Arbeiters"), which can be found in *Poetry and Prose: Bertolt Brecht* (German Library), eds. Reinhold Grimm and Caroline Molina Y Vedia, trans. Michael Hamburger (London: Continuum International Publishing Group, 2003), p. 62.

23. The term *destructive entitlement* was coined by family systems therapist Ivan Boszormenyi-Nagy (see www.psychologytoday.com/articles/199303/here-eternity for a short interview with this therapist about his development of the concept). He and coauthor Barbara R. Krasner amply illustrate the term in *Between Give and Take: A Clinical Guide to Contextual Therapy* (New York: Brunner/Mazel, 1986). I was surprised to learn that Boszormenyi-Nagy was significantly influenced by Jewish theologian and philosopher Martin Buber and Buber's idea of dialogical existence—that life is an encounter and a conversation with everything and everyone including self, others, the transcendent, and even inanimate objects. Boszormenyi-Nagy and Geraldine M. Spark, *Indivisible Loyalties: Reciprocity in Intergenerational Family Therapy* (New York: Brunner/Mazel, 1984), p. 6. In a related but somewhat different vein from the theory of destructive entitlement, contemporary social psychologists Carol Tavris and Elliot Aronson note that justifying a first hurtful act sets the stage for more aggression, and they quote the answer given by the fictional Fyodor Pavlovitch in *The Brothers Karamazov* when asked why he hated someone so much: "He has done me no wrong. But I played him a dirty trick, and ever since I have hated him." Tavris and Aronson, *Mistakes Were Made (but Not by Me): Why We Justify Foolish Beliefs, Bad Decisions, and Hurtful Acts* (Orlando, FL: Harcourt, 2007), pp. 26–28. See also Steven Fein and Steven J. Spencer, "Prejudice as Self-

Image Maintenance: Affirming the Self through Derogating Others," *Journal of Personality and Social Psychology* 73 (1997), pp. 31–44.

24. Questions far more sophisticated, discerning, and trenchant than mine about the past, present, and future of Israel have been asked by Israeli historian and journalist Gershom Gorenberg in *The Unmaking of Israel* (New York: HarperCollins, 2011). The author's educated passion and concern for his country and for Palestinian Arabs make this one of the most balanced and compelling books ever written about Israel. In thinking of my own vision of justice for Palestinians, I was reminded of a beautiful lithograph that a friend gave me when I was sworn in. It hung in my office until the day I retired and bore the words from Deuteronomy 16:20, "Justice, justice shalt thou pursue." This commandment was given to the Israelites as one of many corollaries to the Ten Commandments, and rabbis have often noted that the initial repetition *(tzedek tzedek)* of the Hebrew word for justice is intended to draw our attention to the doubly imperative nature of this requirement as well as to a more in-depth consideration of the dimensions of justice itself. I wanted to find out how this verse appears in non-Jewish translations of the Hebrew Bible, so I turned to www.biblegateway.com, a useful website for anyone interested in Hebrew or Christian scriptures. It provides more than thirty-five different English-language translations of the Bible that can be viewed in parallel format. Some of the translations of Deuteronomy 16:20 are these: "Follow that which is altogether just" (Amplified Bible); "Righteousness! Pursue righteousness" (Common English Bible); "Justice, only justice, you shall follow" (English Standard Version); and, "Right is right, and ever thou must keep it in view" (Knox Bible) (website accessed October 15, 2011). An

excellent online source for viewing the Jewish Bible *(Tanakh)* in Hebrew and English is www.mechon-mamre.org.

25. These words were part of Dr. King's speech on the steps of the State Capitol in Montgomery, Alabama, on March 25, 1965.

26. This passage appears in *Uncommon Gratitude* (Collegeville, MN: Liturgical Press, 2010), a collection of eighteen reflections written by Joan Chittister and Rowan Williams, the Archbishop of Canterbury. The quoted portion appears at pp. 49–51 in Chittister's essay entitled "Conflict."

27. Janet Kauffman, *Places in the World a Woman Could Walk: Short Stories* (New York: Alfred A. Knopf, 1983).

28. Judith Lewis Herman, *Trauma and Recovery: The Aftermath of Violence—from Domestic Abuse to Political Terror* (New York: BasicBooks, 1992), pp. 214–36. This foundational work by a teaching and clinical psychiatrist who is both scholarly and compassionate remains a classic in the field of complex trauma disorders. Psychologist James W. Pennebaker has also studied the role and use of writing in overcoming the effects of trauma. Pennebaker, *Opening Up: The Healing Power of Expressing Emotions*, rev. ed. (New York: The Guilford Press, 1997), pp. 26–42, 89–103.

29. In her dense and complicated book *The Body in Pain: The Making and Unmaking of the World* (New York: Oxford University Press, 1985), scholar Elaine Scarry notes the linguistic difficulty of expressing physical pain. When we talk about most of our interior states, they are usually coupled with a preposition and an object, such as love *for* X, or fear *of* Y, or ambivalence *about* Z. But "physical pain—unlike any other state of consciousness—has no referential content. It is not *of* or *for* anything. It is precisely because it takes no object that it, more than any other phenomenon, resists objectification in language." Scarry, pp. 3–5.

30. Susan Brownmiller, *Against Our Will: Men, Women, and Rape* (New York: Simon and Schuster, 1975).

31. Marilyn French, *The Women's Room* (New York: Simon and Schuster, 1977), p. 433.

32. Anthony Dworkin, Roy Gutman, David Rieff, eds., *Crimes of War 2.0: What the Public Should Know,* rev. ed. (New York: W. W. Norton, 2007).

33. See, e.g., Dean Hamer, *The God Gene: How Faith Is Hardwired into Our Genes* (New York: Doubleday, 2004); Bruce Lipton, *The Biology of Belief: Unleashing the Power of Consciousness, Matter, and Miracles* (Carlsbad, CA: Hay House, 2008); Andrew Newberg, Eugene D'Aquili, and Vince Rause, *Why God Won't Go Away* (New York: Ballantine Books, 2001).

34. The poem can be found in *William Wordsworth: Selected Poems,* ed. Stephen Gill (London: Penguin Classics, 2005), p. 157.

35. Retirement allowed me to begin "listening to teachers and looking into quietness," and it taught me that "only when I stop collecting evidence do the stones begin to speak." First quote: Gerald May, *Simply Sane* (New York: Crossroad Publishing, 1977), p. 96. Second quote: Mark Nepo, *The Book of Awakening: Having the Life You Want by Being Present to the Life You Have* (York Beach, ME: Conari Press, 2000), p. 310.

36. Benjamin Iobst, *Seven Metals: Singing Bowls of Tibet* (Seven Metals Records, 1999), compact disc.

Other Sources

The italicized sections on the dedication page and on the last page of text are my own words. The other brief English-language epigraphs that appear in italics throughout have been included only for illustration and as food for thought. I have attempted to find the primary source of each quotation, but in many instances I have been successful in locating only the secondary source in which I found the excerpt. The available sources I have found are listed below in the order in which they appear in the book, along with a bit of commentary about each one. Websites referenced here and in the preceding list of endnotes were valid at the time of publication, but due to the fluid nature of the Internet, some addresses, as well as the relevance of their contents, may have changed.

Eudora Welty was a distinctly Southern author who lived all her life in Mississippi and died in 2001 at the age of ninety-two. She wrote short stories, novels, and essays and won the Pulitzer Prize for fiction in 1973. Even though I have read most of her work, it was not until I was tracking down the source of the quotation that I discovered she was also a talented photographer. The quotation is from an essay she wrote to accompany a book of her photographs, *One Time, One Place: Mississippi in the Depression: A Snapshot Album*, rev. ed. (Jackson, MS: University Press of Mississippi, 1996), p. 12.

Rainer Maria Rilke was a Bohemian-Austrian author who died in 1926 at the age of fifty-one. His poetry and lyrical prose were written in both German and French and evince his interest in understanding and communicating with what is transcendent. As modern inquiries into spirituality have increased, Rilke's writings have been translated and circulated ever more widely. His most well-known prose work is *Letters to a Young Poet*. The quotation I have used is from the poem "Ninth Duino Elegy," which can be found in *Duino Elegies and The Sonnets to Orpheus*, ed. and trans. Stephen Mitchell, 1st Vintage International edition (New York: Vintage Books, 2009), pp. 55–59.

Lamentations Rabbah is part of the enormous body of rabbinic literature within Judaism. In the context of such literature, *rabbah* usually means "great commentary." This particular tractate is thought to have been written in the seventh century CE, and it generally treats the book of Lamentations in the Hebrew Bible as a mourning for the destruction of the first and second Temples in Jerusalem and for the accompanying dissolution of the Israelites as a cohesive people.

Dorothee Sölle was a German-born liberation theologian who lived from 1929 to 2003. She became politically active in the 1960s, was an outspoken critic of the Vietnam War and of inequalities in impoverished countries, and referred to fundamentalists as "Christofascists." I found this quotation of hers in Matthew Fox's book *Creation Spirituality: Liberating Gifts for the Peoples of the Earth* (New York: HarperCollins, 1991), p. 20.

The verses of the beatitudes in the New Testament book of **Matthew** are from the New International Version of the Bible.

The version of the scripture from the Old Testament book of **Leviticus** is the translation offered by the modern-day and highly readable Jerusalem Bible that has been used in the Roman Catholic Church since 1996. In the Hebrew Bible—and presumably in the hundreds of translations of it into English and other languages and vernaculars—we are commanded no less than thirty-six times to love the stranger.

Julia Alvarez was born in New York City but returned with her parents to the Dominican Republic when she was three months old. She came back to the United States with them in 1960 when she was ten. A frequent theme of many of her poems, novels, and essays is cultural attitudes toward Latina women. The line I have quoted is from her poem "Bilingual Sestina" in *The Oxford Book of Caribbean Verse* (Oxford: Oxford University Press, 2005), p. 252.

Theodore Roethke (1908–1963) was an American poet who struggled for many years with alcoholism and bipolar disorder. He wrote sensitively and imagistically about nature, and he won both the Pulitzer Prize and the National Book Award for poetry. The quotation is the opening line in his poem "In a Dark Time," which can be found in *Theodore Roethke: Selected Poems*, ed. Edward Hirsch (New York: Doubleday Broadway Publishing Group, 2005), p. 116.

Gene Knudsen Hoffman was a Quaker peace activist and pastoral counselor who died in 2010 at the age of ninety-one. One of her many lasting legacies is the Compassionate Listening Project, a nonprofit organization that teaches heart-based skills for building peace in families, communities, workplaces, and the world. The motto of the project is "An enemy is one whose story we have not heard," and a well-designed website offers a glimpse into the breadth and depth of the project's work. See www.compassionatelistening. org. I found the Hoffman quotation in Mark Nepo's *The Book of Awakening* (cited above in endnote 35) on p. 324.

Aeschylus was a Greek poet and dramatist who wrote the play *Agamemnon* in the fifth century BCE. The quotation I have used is widely circulated and is often recognized as having been included in Robert F. Kennedy's announcement about the death of Dr. Martin Luther King Jr. in 1968.

Next to the Torah, the **Talmud** is the main text of Judaism and contains the opinions of thousands of rabbis about hundreds of topics central to the history, beliefs, and practices of the faith. Most of it was written between the third and sixth centuries CE, much of it is in Aramaic, and in printed form it is more than six thousand pages in length. The entirety of the five-sentence quotation I have used is *not* in the Talmud but is popularly attributed to it. The second, third, and fourth sentences are clearly reminiscent of the admonition in Micah 6:8 to do justly, love mercy, and walk humbly with God. The fifth sentence is from that part of the Talmud called *Pirkei Avot* (Ethics of the Fathers), 2:21. The first sentence, however, appears to be the kind of gentle admonition toward right behavior that can be found throughout wisdom literature from many traditions. I have used the quotation as a whole, even though it is a mixture of several things, because I have always found it to be motivating and encouraging.

About the Author

Susan L. Yarbrough is a native Texan who grew up in Dallas. She received a BA degree in English and history from Baylor University, attended graduate school there and at Rice University, worked for a year as a VISTA volunteer, and earned a JD from the University of Houston school of law. After passing the Texas and New York bar exams, she practiced law for nine years in the state and federal trial and appellate courts of New York, where she worked as an attorney for the New York Legal Aid Society and for the New York Attorney General.

Upon returning to Texas, Susan practiced federal criminal appellate law for three years in the office of the United States Attorney for the Southern District of Texas. In 1987, she was appointed to a judgeship on the United States Immigration Court, where she heard a wide variety of cases for almost eighteen years. Since receiving her undergraduate degree, she has taught courses at the college level and has also worked extensively as a licensed massage therapist.

Susan now lives in Texas, enjoys retirement, and uses the gifts of time and age for reading, writing, walking, swimming, gardening, volunteering, and being with friends whose wit and kindness and blessings cannot be described in any known words.